⇢ *The Search for Thomas F. Ward,*
  Teacher of Frederick Delius ⇠

DON C. GILLESPIE

University Press of Florida

Gainesville   Tallahassee   Tampa   Boca Raton   Pensacola   Orlando   Miami   Jacksonville

The Delius Trust has provided a substantial subsidy toward the publication of this volume.
The Trust is a charity registered in England which, since 1935, has supported the performance,
recording, and publication of the music of Frederick Delius.

01   00   99   98   97   96   6   5   4   3   2   1

Library of Congress Cataloging-in-Publication Data
Gillespie, Don C.
The search for Thomas F. Ward, teacher of Frederick Delius / Don C. Gillespie.
p. cm.
Includes bibliographical references and index.
ISBN 0-8130-1398-4 (cloth: alk. paper)
1. Ward, Thomas F. 2. Music teachers—United States—Biography. 3. Organists—United States—
Biography. 4. Delius, Frederick, 1862–1934. I. Title.
ML423.W297G55   1996
780'.92—dc20
[B]   95-44706

The University Press of Florida is the scholarly publishing agency for the State University System
of Florida, comprised of Florida A & M University, Florida Atlantic University, Florida International
University, Florida State University, University of Central Florida, University of Florida, University
of North Florida, University of South Florida, and University of West Florida.

University Press of Florida
15 Northwest 15th Street
Gainesville, FL 32611

In memoriam

Hugh Hodgson

Yes my brother I know,
The rest might not, but I have treasur'd every
    note,
For more than once dimly down to the beach
    gliding,
Silent, avoiding the moonbeams, blending myself
    with the shadows,
Recalling now the obscure shapes, the echoes,
    the sounds and sights after their sorts,
The white arms out in the breakers tirelessly
    tossing,
I, with bare feet, a child, the wind wafting my hair,
Listen'd long and long.
Listen'd to keep, to sing, now translating the
    notes,
Following you my brother.

        WALT WHITMAN (FROM "SEA DRIFT")

Why faintest thou? I wander'd till I died.
Roam on! The light we sought is shining still.
Our tree yet crowns the hill,
Our Scholar travels yet the loved hillside.

        MATTHEW ARNOLD (FROM "THYRSIS")

Contents

Foreword

Eric Fenby

No matter what the motive, withdrawal from the world, if even for a brief period, has usually been the first step that an individual has taken on the road to high endeavor.

In Paris in the 1890s, at times of tremendous inner conflict, Frederick Delius would pack his bag and lose himself in the countryside for weeks together, thinking only of his work; when he could bear that no longer, he would return to Paris and plunge again into the whirlpool of life. Not that he was lazy. The habit of regular work that he had acquired from Thomas Ward in Florida earlier never left him. That virtue was the surest defense against a headstrong nature and hot-blooded temperament such as his, and it saved him.

Speaking of those early days in Florida, Delius once said to me, "Ward's counterpoint lessons were the only lessons from which I ever derived any benefit. He showed wonderful insight in helping me to find out just how much in the way of traditional technique would be useful to me."

I remember my amusement at Grez-sur-Loing when, on turning over the pages of an illustrated edition of the complete works of Byron bearing the inscription "From Thomas F. Ward, Jacksonville, Florida, to Fritz Delius, Leipsic, Germany," I found the following passage heavily scored and marked by a pressed flower:

> The youth who trains, or runs a race,
> Must bear privations with unruffled face
> Be call'd to labour when he thinks to dine,
> And, harder still, leave wenching, and his wine.

Delius was a very fortunate man in most respects. It was always his good luck to meet precisely the very people he needed at the crucial stages of his career. First came Ward, who gave him a sound grounding in his art; then Edvard Grieg, who encouraged him with his friendship and practical advice, and to whom he continued to send his scores for comment after he had left Leipzig; and then Jelka Rosen, to whom he was suitably mated, and who made it materially possible for him to devote himself entirely to composition; and lastly, Thomas Beecham, who did everything that a man could do to establish his genius.

Sadly, Ward himself did not live to see his pupil become famous but died in obscurity. I am thrilled beyond words by Don Gillespie's unique achievement in so successfully and finally solving the mystery of Thomas Ward's unhappy end, and I commend his singular tenacity of purpose in what seemed an almost impossible trail.

Acknowledgments

In gathering materials about Thomas F. Ward's life, I became indebted to many persons (friends and strangers alike), libraries, educational institutions, and religious organizations. The following is only a partial listing of the people who have assisted me over a seven-year span of time.

I am especially grateful to the trustees of the Delius Trust, London, and to its advisers for their support of this project. Their generous assistance has been indispensable for the completion and publication of this book.

From abroad, Lionel Carley, archivist of the Delius Trust, has provided valuable suggestions and immense scholarly authority since our first discussion of the "Ward project" in 1986. His friendship and openness to a fledgling Delius researcher have been crucial. Eric Fenby searched his memory about Ward to provide a direct link through time to Frederick Delius himself. Robert Threlfall, Roger J. Buckley, and Ronald Stevenson all assisted with biographical and musical questions.

Professor H. Wiley Hitchcock, director of the Institute for Studies in American Music at Brooklyn College, early in my research provided intellectual support for what must have seemed to others an unconventional, even shaky foundation upon which to build a musicological study. His editorial advice for the first two chapters was invaluable.

From the Delius Association of Florida in Jacksonville came the valued assistance of Jeff Driggers of the Jacksonville Public Library; Thomas Gunn, director of the Swisher Library at Jacksonville University; and Frank Lieber, who aided in my research and often provided shelter for a stranded and near penurious gypsy scholar.

With kindness and good humor, Stewart Manville, archivist, and Rolf Stang, president, of the Percy Grainger Society in White Plains, New York, lent me

their expertise on both Grainger and Delius. Other scholars from many fields provided beneficial and timely assistance. Professor James J. Horgan, St. Leo College, Florida, shared his research notes for his centennial history of St. Leo College and Monastery and generously provided documents, photographs, and—not least—advice that saved me from ecclesiastical pitfalls. From his earlier research on Delius in Florida, Professor William P. Randel of Alfred, Maine, provided his valuable newspaper references concerning Ward, thus allowing me to postpone an arduous trek through the Jacksonville daily newspapers of a century ago and better use my limited travel time in the South elsewhere.

Others have played a more personal part in this story and have shared my discoveries and disappointments. Robert Beckhard provided not only his expert photographic skills but, as a true Warlockian and Delian, constantly offered his friendship, patiently challenged my premises, and with unwavering enthusiasm helped me develop my sometimes ill-formed ideas about Thomas Ward. His wife Patricia's professional editorial skills have saved me from numerous embarrassments in my struggle with the blank page. Sabine Matthes accompanied me to the wilds of both the St. Johns River and Brooklyn, as well as to the French Quarter of New Orleans and the skyscrapers of Houston, always photographing beautiful scenes, making new friends, and sharing city- and landscapes in our search for "Thomas." Monica Raybon assisted in my research in Brooklyn and shared a journey to Jacksonville and St. Augustine in August 1986, in which Thomas Ward's mystery suddenly became very real to both of us. The late John Cage's interest in the fate of the "Alligator Man," as he called Ward, led me to the certainty that chance, too, would play a part in the story. My good friends Elizabeth Speight and Jan Coward of Philadelphia listened for hours to the Ward saga, always suggesting new directions. Thank you, Jan, for your many photographic missions!

For their support, counsel, and assistance, I must not omit Eugene M. Becker, Frank Billack, Marcia Eckert, Cole Gagne, Joseph Smith, and Dr. Wayne Swift, New York City; Professor Edward R. Reilly, Vassar College; Dan Broucek, Pittsburgh, Pennsylvania; William Duckworth, Lewisburg, Pennsylvania; Vera McFarland and Jo Meldrim, Solano Grove, Florida; Daryl Joseph, Jacksonville; Joseph Manucy, Phyllis Ridge, Jo Bozard, and John C. Redmond, St. Augustine; Alberta Sanks, Picolata; Mark Stoneman, Gainesville; Anthony P. Pizzo and Lucy O'Brien, Tampa; Joseph Spilmann Jr., New Orleans; Carl Cunningham, Pat DeLucia, Leland A. Dolan, and Tom Johnson, Houston;

Marjorie Blaskower, Greenbrae, California; Norman F. Loretz and Norma J. Loretz, San Diego; Nicolas Slonimsky, Los Angeles; Jack P. F. Gremillion III, Statesboro, Georgia; and Vincent Plush, Sydney, Australia.

I owe special debts of gratitude to many other individuals and their scholarly institutions. In New York I should like to thank the following: Arthur Konop, City of Brooklyn Archives of St. Francis College; Claire M. Lamers, Brooklyn Historical Society; Elizabeth White, Brooklyn Collection, Brooklyn Public Library; Richard Jackson, Americana Collection, New York Public Library; Adria Quinones, New-York Historical Society; Charles Young, Queensborough Public Library; Leslie Pasch, Little Falls (New York) Public Library; Judy Haven, Onondaga Historical Association, Syracuse, New York.

In the Deep South and elsewhere: Carol Harris, Florida Collection, Jacksonville Public Library; Jacqueline Fretwell and Jean Trapido, St. Augustine Historical Society; Stephen Kerber, P. K. Yonge Library of Florida History, University of Florida, Gainesville; Elizabeth Jones and John H. Baxley, Hillsborough County Historical Commission, Tampa; Kurt E. Jasielonis, Hillsborough (Tampa) Public Library; Paul Eugen Camp, Library of the University of South Florida, Tampa; Frank Mendola, Orange County History Museum, Orlando; Collin B. Hamer, New Orleans Public Library; Alfred Lemmon, Historic New Orleans Collection; Art Carpenter, Loyola University; Patricia L. Meador, Louisiana State University Library in Shreveport; Joan Dobson, Dallas Public Library; Douglas Weiskopf and Violet Johnson, Houston Public Library; Rosemary Florimell, Grainger Museum, University of Melbourne.

The many wonderful people and institutions of the Catholic faith have enriched my experience beyond words and have provided the main part of this text about a deeply religious man. I would like to thank especially Rev. Harry M. Culkin, Diocesan archivist, Roman Catholic Diocese of Brooklyn; Father John M. Young, archivist, and Brother Emmett Corry of the Franciscan Brothers, St. John's University, Queens; Sister Margaret Quinn, archivist, St. Joseph Convent, Brentwood, New York; Sister Anne Courtney, archivist, Sisters of Charity, Mount St. Vincent on Hudson, Bronx; Father Gabriel Real, St. Paul's Church, Brooklyn; Rt. Rev. Monsignor Charles E. Diviney, St. Charles Borromeo's Church, Brooklyn; Father Gerald Barbarito, Chancery staff, Diocese of Brooklyn; Father Stephen Strouse, St. John the Baptist Church, Brooklyn; Father Sylvester Benack, Church of the Assumption, Brooklyn; Father Dennis Corrado, St. James Cathedral, Brooklyn; Rev. Monsignor Agustin Ruiz, Church of SS. Peter and Paul, Brooklyn; Dr. Mary Wolfe, Office of Catholic

Education, Diocese of Brooklyn; Diane Valek, St. Joseph Children's Services, Brooklyn; Brother Thomas Traeger, St. John's Home for Boys, Rockaway Park, Queens.

In Florida I owe an enormous debt to Father Henry F. Riffle, O.S.B., former archivist of St. Leo Abbey, who trusted my research from the first and who, with faith in the seriousness of this project, never failed to assist me as a fellow scholar. A similar debt is owed to both Rev. Thomas H. Clancy, S.J., archivist, Society of Jesus, Louisiana, and Father Paschal M. Baumstein, O.S.B., archivist, Belmont Abbey, North Carolina. I would also like to express my deep appreciation to the following individuals: Abbot Patrick Shelton, O.S.B.; Rt. Rev. Marion Bowman, O.S.B.; Father Leo Schlosser, O.S.B.; and Brother Joachim Svetlosky, O.S.B., all of St. Leo Abbey; Martha Hendren and Sheila Fava, Office of the Abbot, Belmont Abbey; Brother Philip Hurley, O.S.B., archivist, St. Vincent Archabbey, Latrobe, Pennsylvania; Father Michael F. Kennelly, S.J., Church of the Sacred Heart, Tampa; Father Philip R. Gagan, archivist, Diocese of St. Augustine; Father Gilbert Wolters, O.S.B., archivist, St. Benedict's Abbey, Atchison, Kansas; Monsignor Teodoro de la Torre, Annunciation Church, Houston, Texas; Sister Mary E. Sheridan, Sisters of Mercy, Macon, Georgia.

Finally, to Sister Mary Albert Lussier of St. Augustine, archivist of the Sisters of St. Joseph in Florida, I owe the largest debt of all. No amount of delving into obscure and arcane documents would have produced a true portrait of Ward without her help. With her deep knowledge of Florida's religious past and her religious order's own historical links to Thomas Ward, which were gradually revealed, she came to understand his Catholic character almost as if she were his contemporary. She was, in fact, a co-voyager in my search for Thomas F. Ward, and her invaluable interpretations, intuitions, and encouragements helped keep me on a path of discovery whose direction was sometimes uncertain and often stalemated.

To the Sisters of St. Joseph everywhere, I hope that I have in some way repaid, on behalf of Thomas F. Ward, an ancient debt owed to their charity and selflessness.

"A most charming fellow into the bargain."

Many years ago, as an undergraduate at the University of Georgia in Athens, I wandered over to the library one Friday evening to listen to some music. For no particular reason except for the strange record jacket—a picture of a cabin in a swamp, some cypress trees, and hanging moss—I picked a piece by Frederick Delius entitled *Appalachia: Variations on an Old Slave Song*, for chorus and orchestra. I read the evocative text of the song whose origin even to this day is unknown to folklorists. It was a song of separation and hope:

> O Honey, I am going down the river in the morning,
> Heigh ho, heigh ho, down the mighty river;
> Aye! Honey, I'll be gone when next the whippoorwill's a calling,
> And don't you be too lonesome love,
> And don't you fret and cry;
> For the Dawn will soon be breaking
> The radiant morn is nigh.
> And you'll find me ever awaiting, my own sweet Nellie Gray!
> To'rds the morning lift a voice;
> Let the scented woods rejoice
> And echoes swell across the mighty stream!

At the end of the song, as if words could no longer express the intense identification of the voices with nature, the chorus bursts into an inexpressibly beautiful cry of rapture. I have never forgotten the impression which that music made on me—a lonesome music student from a little south Georgia town. It did not suggest the red clay hills of Athens, or the dark brown Oconee River of north Georgia, but instead, clear streams, sultry evenings, marshes,

Frederick Delius, *Appalachia*. Two excerpts from the vocal score. (Harmonie Verlag, 1907. By permission of Boosey & Hawkes, Ltd.)

a never-ending forest of pine trees. The inner voices of the chromatic harmonies seemed improvised, moving according to no specific rules, appearing awkward on the page but sounding unalterably right. In a word, it sounded southern: it was the special world of south Georgia and north Florida. It was home!

I immediately wanted to know everything about the romantic composer who could write such a work, and so I took the discovery to my piano teacher,

Hugh Hodgson—"Mr. Hugh," as his students affectionately called him. He was the founder of the music department at the university and a legendary figure from one of Athens's aristocratic families.

Mr. Hugh had two casual observations that both shocked and intrigued me. First he said, "Isn't it awful what happened to Delius? The terrible way he died?" And then, "You know, he learned to compose from someone down on an orange plantation in Florida. Thomas Ward was his name, from Brooklyn. Nobody knows what ever became of Mr. Ward. Isn't that the strangest thing you ever heard?"

I am paraphrasing Mr. Hugh at a distance of more than three decades, but I have always wondered how he knew these things. I didn't know then that Delius had suffered an agonizing death from syphilis in 1934 in France, much less that he had been profoundly influenced in the early 1880s in Florida by the South and by a Brooklyn organist named Thomas F. Ward.

Fascination with Delius's music and its origins in the Old South followed me through the 1960s. In 1969, I searched out Solano Grove, Delius's Florida plantation, located forty miles below Jacksonville on the St. Johns River, where the river is more than three miles wide. The remains of a giant oak tree from Delius's and Ward's time were still in the woods in one of the most tranquil scenes of nature I had ever viewed.

I had gone to Jacksonville from the University of North Carolina in Chapel Hill in search of a dissertation topic about Delius and Ward in Florida, but the search at that time came to nothing, and I abandoned it. Yet I never forgot that feeling of peace and closeness to nature on the bank of the St. Johns River. It remained a mantra in my hectic professional life in music publishing in New York City in the 1970s and kept beckoning me to return. After a fifteen-year interruption, an academic dissertation (on another subject) long in hand, it occurred to me that, being a New Yorker now, I could pick up the trail again and go to Brooklyn to find out whether there were any remaining traces of the mysterious Thomas Ward, even though earlier the tracks in Florida had led nowhere.

That is the background for what became in the ensuing years a total obsession: Who was Thomas F. Ward? Where did he come from? What happened to him? And most important, how could one person have such a profound influence on another, and yet the one's path (Delius's) led to musical immortality and the other's (Ward's) to historical oblivion? It seemed so unfair, a romantic, haunting image that would not fade away.

Solano Grove, July 1989. (Photo by Sabine Matthes.)

We might now ask: What exactly is the point in spending years in attempting to resurrect the American teacher of Frederick Delius? Why would one invest such an enormous amount of time on such a seemingly unimportant musicological project? Reactions to my project have varied from bemused puzzlement to shared excitement. On December 18, 1986, the legendary music lexicographer Nicolas Slonimsky answered a letter of mine with the query: "What on earth possessed you to travel all over the land in search of the teacher of Delius? Who cares? Anyway, I for one do not intend to follow in your footsteps in the marshes of Florida or search for his remains in the cemeteries." (But he then offered some valuable genealogical advice.) The opposite reaction came from the great Delius scholar and his amanuensis, Eric Fenby, on June 30, 1986: "I have been waiting half a century for the letter you sent me on Thomas Ward. . . . Your intensive researches into what happened to him prove you to be the one man likely to solve this mystery. You have my full support." He added: "It is a hundred years this month since Delius and Ward parted. Clearly, Delius regretted having lost touch with him."

I confess that I accept the premise that the American influence on Delius's career and music may have been the most important one—more decisive than that of Edvard Grieg, which followed, or the various currents of mod-

ernism that Delius encountered in Europe on his return from America and eventual settlement in France. It is my belief that Delius would not have become the composer we know today had he not encountered Ward and that certainly the direction his music would have taken without Ward and Florida would have been quite different; it would have been much less original without the mélange of American and European influences that underlies his special sound world.

Only a few facts were known about Thomas F. Ward in the mid-1980s when I began this project. I have accepted only those statements that derive directly from Delius himself, for where Ward is concerned the tendency to embellish and fantasize has been irresistible to most writers.

Interestingly, Ward's name does not occur at all in the first scholarly work on Delius, a brief monograph in German by Max Chop published in 1907 when Delius's music was gaining wide acceptance in Germany.[1] Chop alludes to the exotic atmosphere of Florida (*Appalachia*, alligator hunting, black servants, etc.) but does not mention Ward. Perhaps the full Florida story was too personal to be revealed to an objective German *Musikwissenschaftler*—to a stranger.

Nor is Ward mentioned in the lengthy and perceptive biographical portrait of Delius by the American composer Edward Burlingame Hill in 1909, shortly before Delius's first important American premiere: the performance of *Paris* by the Boston Symphony Orchestra under Max Fiedler on November 26, 1909. On the contrary, Hill informs us that in Florida Delius "pursued his musical studies *alone*" while reflecting upon the tradition of the great masters of the past.[2]

Strangely, the first known reference to Ward and Delius appears not in Europe, where Delius was well known, but in New York City, where his music was a still a novelty. On the occasion of the American premiere of Delius's Piano Concerto in New York City on November 26, 1915, by the Australian pianist Percy Grainger, H. E. Krehbiel, the eminent music critic of the *New York Tribune*, mentioned a "New York organist" who had strongly influenced Delius's music:

> [Delius] wanted to be a musician, his father wanted him to be a merchant, and as a sort of compromise he was sent to Florida, when he arrived at his majority, to manage an orange grove which his father had bought for him. In Florida he "studied music and nature," guided in the

former study by a New York organist, who had gone to Florida for his health. This organist, whose name has not been confided to us, lived on Delius's orange grove for several months, and as a recent English sketch puts it, "imparted to his host all the musical technique that can be taught in a place where practical experience is impossible." (November 21, 1915)

I have not yet identified the written "recent English sketch" from which Krehbiel might have drawn his remarks. Perhaps the source was an oral one. Unquestionably, this information must have come from Percy Grainger himself, who had recently moved from London to New York. The famous composer-pianist was an intimate friend of Delius and an enthusiastic proponent of his music in America. In late 1915 Grainger was, in fact, making zealous propaganda for both Delius's Piano Concerto and for his own appearance with the New York Philharmonic in Carnegie Hall. Only to his closest musical colleague would Delius have suggested that the name of Ward not be "confided." But why?

Thomas F. Ward's name first appears in the 1923 study of Delius by Philip Heseltine (alias Peter Warlock), as remembered by the composer almost forty years after his Florida experience. There we read the story of the chance meeting in 1884 of young Fritz Delius the would-be orange grower, sent to Florida to escape the lure of music, and Tom Ward, the new organist of Jacksonville's Catholic Church, in Merryday & Paine's music store on West Bay Street near the Jacksonville waterfront. I will quote Heseltine in some detail, as his account touches on an area of controversy concerning Ward's Brooklyn background. The words of Heseltine, an intimate friend of Delius and worshipper of his music—and a master of the English language—sound a bit like scripture:

> Now, it happened that while he [Delius] was trying one of the pianos that were offered to him, there passed by the open door of the shop an individual who was so struck by the beauty of the sounds proceeding from inside that he came in and begged to be made acquainted with the young man who was playing. This individual was Thomas F. Ward, organist of the Jesuit Church of SS. Peter and Paul in Brooklyn, the son of a Spanish priest and an Irish kitchen-maid. He was inclined to consumption and had been sent by the Fathers of his Church to the South in the hope of restoring his health. It was a romantic encounter. A lively sympathy between the two musicians led to their returning together to the orange grove with the

piano. Ward was an excellent musician . . . and it is not too much to say that the whole of Delius's technical equipment is derived from the instruction he received from Ward in the course of his six months' sojourn on the plantation. The young composer developed very rapidly. He worked with a demoniacal energy, and in a short time he had as good a knowledge of musical technique as the average student at the institutions acquires in the course of two or three years. In his teaching, Ward wisely confined himself to counterpoint, seeing that his pupil's natural instincts had already provided him with a finer sense of harmony than could ever be gained from textbooks and treatises.

Heseltine further asserts that Delius learned even more from Ward's "admirable performance of the great masters—especially Bach, of whom his knowledge equalled his love—on the piano at the plantation and on the organ of a Roman Catholic Church in Jacksonville, which was occasionally visited for this purpose."[3]

The second valid source about Ward is Eric Fenby's memoir of 1936, *Delius as I Knew Him* (the source of Ken Russell's well-known film biography of Delius's last years, *Song of Summer*). According to Fenby, Delius himself related that:

"It was not until I began to attend the harmony and counterpoint classes at the Leipzig Conservatorium that I realized the sterling worth of Ward as a teacher. He was excellent for what I wanted to know, and a most charming fellow into the bargain. Had it not been that there were great opportunities for hearing music and talking music, and that I met Grieg, my studies at Leipzig were a complete waste of time. As far as my composing was concerned, Ward's counterpoint lessons were the only lessons from which I ever derived any benefit. Towards the end of my course with him—and he made me work like a slave—he showed wonderful insight in helping me to find out just how much in the way of traditional technique would be useful to me." After a pause, in which he appeared to be deep in thought, he added, "And there wasn't much. A sense of flow is the main thing, and it doesn't matter how you do it so long as you master it."[4]

Fenby added, "Unhappily, Ward did not live to see his pupil famous, but died of tuberculosis, after spending the last years of his short life in a monastery"—a statement which I eventually discovered to be partially inaccurate.

Ward instilled in Delius the virtues of discipline and hard work at one's profession. "The habit of regular work which he had acquired from Ward, out there in Florida, never left him." Fenby wrote: "Ward, a devout Catholic . . . had known his pupil for what he was—a headstrong, boisterous, hot-blooded young fellow with more than a streak of the adventurer in him—and he had taken him well in hand." This Catholic-instilled discipline was enough to sustain Delius years later, "even amid the thousand and one distractions of Paris," as Fenby expressed it. He regretted that Delius did not take on even more of Ward's Catholic character, "not so much as to make his pupil a Catholic, but at least a believer."[5] Fenby added nothing significant to this portrait of Ward in his later monograph *Delius*,[6] but in 1984 he repeated Delius's account of his American teacher, furnishing a few significant details about Delius's escape to America and his exotic new locale:

"Florida! Ah! Florida! I loved Florida—the people, the country—and the silence! . . . I wanted to get away as far as possible from parental opposition to my becoming a musician. . . . Just think, I met Thomas Ward, an organist, by chance whilst choosing a piano in a Jacksonville music-store! I didn't realize what a good teacher he was until I went eventually to Leipzig Conservatoire. The professors there had no insight whatever compared with his. His instruction was intuitive; just what I needed. He was a fine fellow, too, and I was grieved when he died of consumption some years later.

[At Solano Grove] I used to get up early and be spellbound watching the silent break of dawn over the river; Nature awakening—it was wonderful! At night the sunsets were all aglow—spectacular. Then the coloured folk on neighbouring plantations would start singing instinctively in parts as I smoked a cigar on my verandah."[7]

In response to a hopeful inquiry of mine concerning Ward, Fenby could only offer that he was, according to Delius, "a most endearing man of the highest integrity and personal charm." As Fenby had described him to me, one did not ask questions of Delius; his first interrogation of the composer at Delius's home in Grez-sur-Loing brought a sharp rebuke: "Never ask questions, boy: To answer them is weak!"

The ties between Delius and Ward were apparently severed after 1885. After a year and a half in Florida, Delius left his neglected plantation to his newly arrived brother and, with a letter of recommendation from Tom Ward, moved to Danville, Virginia, in the fall of 1885, where he taught for a while

at a girls' finishing school before returning in June 1886 to Europe and eventual fame.[8] When, in the spring of 1897, Delius returned to Solano Grove during his last trip to America, he heard the news that his friend Ward had died in the mysterious circumstances he later related to Fenby.

No letters between Delius and Ward have survived. Apart from a poem by Ward in one of Delius's music sketchbooks, there exists only a volume of the works of Lord Byron inscribed "From Thomas F. Ward, Jacksonville, Florida, to Fritz Delius, Leipsic, Germany," in which a flower has been pressed. Ward had marked in pencil the following passage from Byron's "Hints from Horace":

> The youth who trains, or runs a race,
> Must bear privations with unruffled face
> Be call'd to labour when he thinks to dine,
> And, harder still, leave wenching, and his wine.[9]

That is the complete record of Ward that can be reliably traced to Delius. All other accounts in which Ward is described, sometimes at length (including those by Delius's sister Clare and by the noted Florida historian Gloria Jahoda), have served only to muddy the waters. Clare Delius recounts, in the midst of much embroidery, that "Fred . . . often told me in after years how he learned more from Mr. Ward than he ever learned from anybody else."[10] Gloria Jahoda, whose contribution to Delius research is in many ways admirable, relates as facts (not as the intuitions they are) how, in company with Delius, Ward's mind raced with talk of Mendelssohn's oratorios, how he told Delius about a pianist named Louis M. Gottschalk, and so on.[11] Another writer, following Jahoda, even reveals that the contents of Delius's first meal down on the plantation consisted of "pork and field peas"![12]

Deems Taylor (1885–1966), the popular American composer, writer, and radio commentator, provided possibly the most fanciful account of the two musicians' encounter. In his best-selling 1937 music appreciation text *Of Men and Music*, an uncharacteristically shy Delius and an unusually loquacious Ward made an appearance in a book that by 1945 had gone through twelve printings and 47,000 copies:

> "I hope you'll forgive the intrusion," [Ward] said, "but as I was coming up the street I heard someone playing in here; and I don't hear many good pianists in this part of the country. I had to come in and find out who it

was. Besides, I'm very curious about that music. I'm pretty familiar with organ and piano music, but that piece you were just playing is absolutely new to me. What is it?"

The young man [Delius] seemed a little embarrassed. "Why . . . er," he stammered, "it's . . . it's really nothing at all. I was just improvising."

Ward, whose interest by this time was beginning to border on excitement, began to ask questions.[13]

The romanticizing of the Delius-Ward story, plus the scant facts available, have caused some reputable scholars to downplay Ward's influence on Delius; among them is the foremost authority on Delius's stay in America, the historian William Randel. But we are forced to consider the fact that Delius never wavered in his assertions about Ward's influence. After a concert in St. Augustine, Florida, the pianist Ethel Bartlett described to a local historian her visit to Delius at Grez toward the end of his life. Delius told her that "there by the St. Johns he had developed traits of character that had been a never failing source of strength all his life" and that he "could not say too much of the debt he owed for the instruction received from [Thomas Ward]."[14] Despite his anti-Christian, often blasphemous stance toward all religions in his later years, Delius never betrayed his friendship with the Catholic friend of his youth, whose religious belief confronted the atheistic young composer head-on in 1884.

Thomas F. Ward, however, remained a blank page: the missing link of Delius's biography. To bring him out of the shadows, to reveal the mysterious musician Delius considered the major influence on his artistic development, and "a most charming fellow into the bargain," we must begin by going back to the nineteenth century.

✦ *Brooklyn*

"A boy of uncommon ability and talent."

We might start by briefly investigating Brooklyn in the 1860s and 1870s when Thomas F. Ward was growing up. From the Church of Saints Peter and Paul, he could have viewed "Gotham" (New York City) and the crowded clipper-ship traffic on the nearby East River. The Great Brooklyn Theatre Fire of 1876, the public's raves for the newly discovered Wagner music dramas and for Gilbert and Sullivan's *H.M.S. Pinafore,* Luciano Conterno's famous Coney Island summer band, the scandalous adultery trial of the "Great Divine" Henry Ward Beecher, the summer "strawberry picnics" of the religious organizations, the July excursions of orphans to Coney Island—all these would have been known to Ward. The Brooklyn Bridge was under construction from 1870 to 1883, and from one of his church posts in downtown Brooklyn Ward would have seen its eastern tower growing daily.

As for music, Brooklyn did not need to bow to New York during that period. The fourth largest city in the country, the "city of churches" had its own rich musical tradition that reflected the domination of German classicism and romanticism in serious music as well as the genteel, cultivated tradition that held sway over nineteenth-century America's musical mores. Ward could have heard the orchestral concerts of Theodore Thomas and the Philharmonic Society at the Academy (then on Montague Street in the "Heights") and the recitals of Anton Rubinstein, Hans von Bülow, the Norwegian fiddler Ole Bull, the organist Dudley Buck, the famous saxophonist Edward Lefêbre, and the celebrated soprano Adelina Patti. He may have been familiar with the compositions of George F. Bristow and Ellsworth C. Phelps, at that time well-known local composers. Had he wished, he could have heard countless concerts of Wagner's music, for which New Yorkers and Brooklynites were developing an almost insatiable appetite.

Ward's name occasionally appears in the pages of the *Brooklyn Eagle* and other contemporary newspapers, church ledgers, and government archives. From these, there gradually emerges a picture of a young man of good moral fiber, firmly devoted to the Catholic faith. There is no evidence that Thomas Ward ever left his native Brooklyn before departing for Florida in 1884. Indeed, documents recently brought to light suggest that he was very much a son of Brooklyn—a genuine Brooklynite.

A casual, chatty letter located not in Brooklyn but in Florida—at the St. Augustine Historical Society—unlocks some of the mysteries of Ward's pre-Florida life and in fact serves as a veritable "Rosetta stone" for investigation into several areas of his youth. The writer was Martha B. Richmond (1884–1968), a prominent Jacksonville socialite who was responsible for awakening local interest in Delius's Florida period. Addressing her St. Augustine friend Kathryn S. Lawson, then director of the local historical society, Mrs. Richmond looked forward in early 1946 to a visit from "Mr. & Mrs. Todd" of Richmond Hill, New York:

[January 24, 1946]

Would long-distance you but am so hoarse can hardly talk, especially on phone.

What news! Will contrive to get there, at least for a day, to meet the Todds. . . . Richmond Hill, L[ong] Island, interests me too. *Thomas Ward's* teacher, was a Prof. Lorentz, of Long Island, a famous teacher of that time.

Thomas Ward and a younger sister were orphans and were at St. John's House, Sisters of St. Joseph, Brooklyn, N.Y., when Mother de Chantal was Mother Superior of the institution—

It would be wonderful if Mr. and Mrs. Todd could run down traces of Thomas Ward, his teacher Lorentz etc, when they go back to Long Island.

The source of Mrs. Richmond's information was probably Mrs. Henry Clark, an acquaintance of hers and a pupil of Thomas Ward's, who in the 1930s still remembered his "courtly manner" and "fine musicianship," according to a brief memo from Mrs. Richmond dated August 1966.[1]

As Mrs. Richmond had discovered, the orphan Thomas Ward was reared in St. John's Home, a Catholic boys' orphanage, by the Sisters of St. Joseph, probably from the age of twelve on—not, however, under the well-known Superior, Mother De Chantal Keating, who came to the orphanage in 1883, but under Mother Mary Baptista Hanson, who took over the direction of the

institution at the time of its construction in 1868.[2] Located at the corner of Albany and St. Mark's Avenues, the magnificent structure of St. John's Home was finally torn down in 1948 when the present Albany Housing Project was constructed and the orphanage removed to Rockaway Park in Queens, where it still functions, though in a much diminished capacity. Few records of the old St. John's Home survive at the current Queens orphanage; all documents prior to the 1890s were apparently lost in a disastrous fire on December 18, 1884, which, according to the *Brooklyn Eagle* of December 19, took the lives of fifteen persons and destroyed half of the structure.

Information buried in federal and state census records (1865 to 1880) offers strong proof that Ward was born either in early 1856 or late 1855. The census records imply that he was not, as some sources state, almost a decade older than Delius (b. 1862), nor a near contemporary, but more of an older brother figure, at most five to six years Delius's senior.[3] He therefore would have been able to exert a comradely, tempering, but nevertheless authoritarian influence on the hedonistic composer-to-be.

Letter from Martha B. Richmond to Kathryn S. Lawson, January 24, 1946. (St. Augustine Historical Society.)

St. John's Home (a Roman Catholic orphan asylum for boys). From Henry R. Stiles, *A History of the City of Brooklyn* (1870). (Brooklyn Historical Society.)

Ward's strong Catholic character can be substantiated in newspaper accounts of his day, where we find confirmation that he not only served as spokesman for the orphans but was also involved with the institution's cultural life—with the musical nurturing and moral training of the younger boys. For example, a local weekly paper, the *Catholic Review*, reported on July 11, 1874, that St. John's Home had recently presented a drama based on the life of Sir Thomas More in which "the music, vocal and instrumental, was excellent" and that it

> reflected the highest credit on Master T. Ward, who trained the boys for this occasion. . . . T. Ward, who personated Sir Thomas More, proved that he fully understood the character of the illustrious statesman represented. He is a boy of uncommon ability and talent. . . . From the little "Cuckoo Song" by the juveniles to the efforts of the more advanced pupils, there was observable the careful training and religious influence which the sisters [of St. Joseph] who have charge of this admirable institution exercise over the children entrusted to their care.

Several other examples of Ward's strong moral concerns exist. The *Brooklyn Eagle* was especially watchful of the city's orphans, reporting that during an especially "jubilant gathering" on St. Joseph's Day, March 20, 1882, before a "large and distinguished audience," including many well-known residents of the city,

Thomas F. Ward . . . delivered a very pleasing address, in which he thanked the officers and managers of the orphan asylum, on behalf of the lady superior and the Sisters of St. Joseph, for their watchfulness, zeal and kindness in the government and management of the institution. Mr. Ward also announced that through sagacious business supervision the entire indebtedness, both floating and bonded, of the asylum had been extinguished, which statement was tremendously applauded. (March 21, 1882)

At a benefit in 1877 at St. John's Home, in which the sisters "were indefatigable in their efforts to promote the comfort and enjoyment of their guests," Ward accompanied the orphans in a selection of popular songs. The presentation won the hearts of a very large attendance and the full sympathy of the press. On June 8, 1877, the *Eagle* noted: "All the pieces were very well rendered and elicited hearty applause. 'Our little ones' who sang 'Riding in a Sleigh,' were about fifty little boys, from four to seven years of age, tastefully dressed in white and wearing broad sashes of bright colored ribbon. Every one of the little fellows looked as though he was some proud mother's darling, so neat and clean and handsomely dressed were they."

The intensity of Thomas Ward's view of himself as an orphan—his closeness to others like himself—seems to be the one thread running through his Brooklyn youth. In the spring of 1879, the famous cornetist Jules Levy visited the orphanage under Ward's musical leadership and presented a concert touchingly reported in the *Brooklyn Eagle* of May 7, under the headline "Levy and the Little Children." For Easter 1875 Ward and his orphan chorus entertained the prisoners at the Kings County Penitentiary, a fact appreciatively noted in the *Brooklyn Union* of March 29. During the Christmas season of 1882 the *Catholic Review* of December 23 described an "exceedingly well rendered 'Hallelujah Chorus'" by Ward and his choir of fifty boys. The "healthy appearance" of the seven hundred boys in the orphanage indicated that "they are well cared for," and the reporter's tour through the "large and well-ventilated dormitories, [with their] clean and neat appearances," revealed that "the good sisters of St. Joseph . . . have the interests of the friendless ones committed to their care closely at heart."

But where was Thomas Ward before he entered the "well-ventilated dormitories" of St. John's Home and came under the care of the good Sisters of St. Joseph? We must look further back in time to find the mysterious circumstances of his birth mentioned by Philip Heseltine—to attempt to discover the Spanish priest and Irish kitchen maid who were his parents.

The first occurrence of Thomas Ward's name. Enumeration of the temporary Roman Catholic orphan asylum for boys. (New York State Census of 1865.)

Exactly when, as a boy, Ward first became aware of the Catholic Church is not known. His name does not appear in the 1860 U.S. Census of the Catholic boys' orphanage, located since 1857 at the corner of Bedford and Willoughby Avenues, under the charge of the Franciscan Brothers. On November 9, 1862, while "a pitiless storm [was] raging," according to a contemporary account, the orphanage on Bedford Avenue was burned to the ground, and "the children were thrown destitute on to the community."[4] After the boys were temporarily rehoused in downtown Brooklyn at the corner of Jay and Chapel Streets, next to St. James Cathedral, Thomas Ward is listed among their number, and he first appears in the 1865 state census enumeration of that institution as "age 10."[5]

Comparing the orphans' situation on Jay Street to their St. John's Home relocation as of 1868, the Brooklyn Catholic describes the "high and healthy part of the city" to which the boys had been transferred and continues: "We all know how cruel necessity obliged the youngsters to be cribbed, cabined, and confined within the narrow limits of the Jay St. house. . . . [At St. John's Home] they have ample room . . . pure air, and plenty of heaven's sunlight, with a gladsome view of the open country, not to speak of the towns and cities spread out in one grand panorama before their eyes" (April 24, 1869).

The newspaper's account of the unhealthy conditions at Jay Street suggests that the origins of Ward's tuberculosis, mentioned by Heseltine and

Temporary Roman Catholic orphan asylum for boys (built in 1857), corner of Jay and Chapel Streets. (Photo by Jan Coward.)

Fenby, lay in the "cribbed, cabined, and confined" conditions in the heart of crowded Brooklyn, where he may have lived for six years.

But where did the four-year-old child live before he became an orphan? Accepting Mrs. Richmond's "Rosetta stone" fact that Ward had a younger sister, I located in the 1870 Brooklyn census a "Mary Ward," aged thirteen, in the Catholic girls' orphanage at the corner of Congress and Clinton Streets, under the care of the Sisters of Charity.[6] I now needed to find a family named Ward with children Thomas and Mary in the 1860 Census, a family moreover that must disappear in later census records. A search through the 1860 Kings County census provided just that: the family of Francis Ward, carpenter, aged forty, and his thirty-year-old wife Rose (listed as Rosa), living at 208 Hamilton Avenue in the Irish neighborhood of Red Hook, with their children Thomas, four, Mary, two, and a two-month-old infant, Cecilia.[7]

Visiting the Catholic churches in that area, I soon found the baptismal records of Mary (b. November 1, 1857) and Cecilia (b. May 18, 1860) at the old church of St. Mary Star of the Sea on Court Street in Carroll Gardens. But no record of Thomas Ward's birth or baptism was to be found. Brooklyn directories revealed that "Francis Ward, carpenter," had earlier lived at 44 Atlantic Avenue in 1857, close to St. Paul's Church, the second oldest Roman Catholic Church in the diocese, its tower dominating the Brooklyn skyline then, as it does the neighborhood of Cobble Hill now. An inquiry there, however, elicited that no Thomas Ward was in its baptismal records; visits in the summer of 1986 to all Brooklyn Catholic Churches in existence before 1860 produced nothing further.

The two central mysteries about Thomas Ward are "where did the Brooklyn orphan come from?" and "what happened to him—where and in what

The family of Francis and Rose Connelly Ward. (U.S. Census of 1860.)

circumstances did his life end?" My investigations about the beginning of his life often led to a clue about the end, and evidence in Florida sometimes pointed back to his Brooklyn origins. With no further evidence available to me in Brooklyn in the summer of 1986, the solution to his birth had to come from the South, from the period *after* Delius left America in 1886, the time in which Ward was said to have entered a monastery.

In the late nineteenth century, only one monastery existed in Florida, the Benedictine priory of St. Leo, founded near Dade City in west central Florida in 1889. In its early years it was under the administration of Maryhelp Abbey in Belmont, North Carolina, near Charlotte. Where else could Ward have gone but there? Inquiries made of St. Leo Abbey and Belmont (formerly Maryhelp) Abbey in 1986 brought the response that no Thomas F. Ward had ever been at either monastery, but there had been a "Peter Ward" at Maryhelp Abbey in 1894, who had left after his novitiate there and had "professed at St. Leo's Priory, Florida."[8] The name was wrong and the date seemed much too late, but was it possible that Ward did not die of consumption in the 1880s, but lived for some time thereafter, and that Peter Ward and Thomas Ward were the same person? An urgent letter to Belmont Abbey requesting that they investigate this possibility brought the following response on July 17, 1986: "Peter Ward and Thomas F. Ward are indeed the same man." In 1894 Ward had chosen the name Peter on beginning his novitiate at the North Carolina monastery. (I also discovered that he later chose still other religious names in Florida, further obscuring his trail.)

Unless a special dispensation is given, a baptismal record and an *Exeat* (a bishop's permission to go to another diocese) are requirements for acceptance into a monastic community; and the archives at Belmont Abbey revealed that the monastery officials had requested Thomas F. Ward's records from St. Paul's Church in Brooklyn. But, despite prodding by the Bishop's House in Brooklyn on behalf of Maryhelp Abbey, the information about Ward was not forthcoming. On June 27, 1894, Charles E. McDonnell, the Bishop of Brooklyn, wrote to Rev. Felix Hintemeyer, O.S.B., of Maryhelp Abbey expressing his puzzlement at not being able to clear up this matter:

> On my return home this evening from an official visit out of town I find your application of the 26th *inst.* for an Exeat for Mr. Thomas F. Ward awaiting me. Up to date I have twice tried to get the necessary information for the filling out of the testimonial and Exeat, but for some reason or another this information has not been sent me. I have been away so often on Visitation recently that I could not urge the matter. I am now sending again for the information and I hope to get it in a day or two.
>
> So far as my own knowledge is concerned I know nothing of the young man.[9]

On July 7 the Bishop again wrote the abbey that the rector of St. Paul's Church "cannot give me any information about the young man" or find any record of him in the baptismal registers of the Church. He continued: "All the testimony I have of the young man is contained in your own letter, and, is the only testimony on which I can give the *litterae testimoniales*. As you are satisfied from your knowledge of him for so many years to receive him into the Order, I have no hesitation in transferring him from his diocese to the jurisdiction of the Order."[10]

Even before receipt of this information, however, the Bishop of St. Augustine, John Moore, on May 22, 1894, had issued a special order to Rev. Charles Mohr, O.S.B., of St. Leo Monastery granting Ward "full permission to enter the Order of St. Benedict."[11] The acquisition of Ward's baptismal record must have become less urgent for St. Leo's. But not for me.

Reasoning that only Thomas F. Ward could have directed the Benedictine authorities to St. Paul's Church for these records, I returned to St. Paul's and appealed for permission from Father Gabriel Real to search personally through the records that had been scanned for me earlier by his staff (and by his own predecessor almost a century ago). Under the date May 1, 1856, I found the

names of Thomas Ward and his parents, listed as Francis and Rose Connelly Ward. The entry, in ink, is at the top of the page, above the first regular listing, with the note "date of baptism uncertain" and with no officiating priest listed. Written in a hand that does not appear in the book again, it is the sole irregular entry in the church's two large volumes covering a ten-year period of baptisms—the only instance in which a priest's name and a date of baptism are absent. It was obviously entered at a later date, and the information seems deliberately not to have been forwarded to Maryhelp Abbey in 1894.

My investigation now quickly led me to the *real* father of Thomas F. Ward— none other than a priest (with a non-Spanish name) to be found in John Sharp's exhaustive listings of the Brooklyn Diocese's priests.[12] Even in 1894, the rector of St. Paul's Church had good reason not to relay the incomplete baptismal record of Thomas F. Ward and any implications that might thus be suggested about the clerics who had preceded him. But what about Delius's

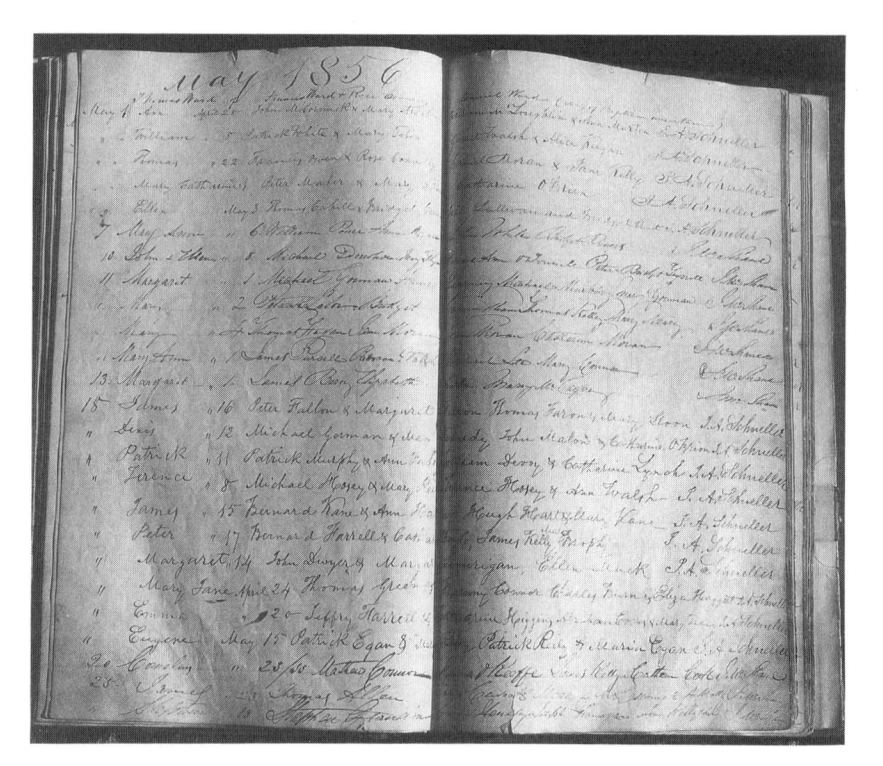

The baptismal record of Thomas Ward, May 1856, St. Paul's Church, Brooklyn. (Photo by Sabine Matthes.)

"Spanish priest," whom we encountered in Heseltine's narrative? There is one plausible solution. Although in no way directly associated with Thomas Ward, Rev. J. A. Schneller, the well-known rector of St. Paul's Church from 1847 to 1861, possessed a flawless command of Spanish, as an examination of the Church's baptismal books verifies. This highly unusual but purely coincidental circumstance probably caused confusion in Ward's own mind as he later attempted to unravel the facts about his parentage. It would have become even more garbled when retold by Delius decades later, resulting in his misleading statement about the "Spanish priest."

I see no reason to reveal the name of Ward's priest-father, who, other evidence shows, quit the active clergy early in 1857 and became listed as "extern" in their ledger—that is, as no longer serving as a priest. We can surmise that he must have left the Church voluntarily to avoid scandal and excommunication. My conclusions are that Francis and Rose Connelly Ward were Thomas Ward's adopted parents, that Francis was a relative of the real father, and that Thomas's sister Mary is not his close blood relative but is the natural child of Francis and Rose—and that the name of Thomas Ward's real mother, the Irish kitchen maid mentioned by Delius to Heseltine, will probably remain shrouded in mystery.

I do not know what catastrophic event disrupted the family of Francis and Rose Connelly and led to Thomas Ward's being placed in an orphanage at the beginning of the Civil War. A search for Francis's name among Civil War casualties and in obituary notices has revealed nothing. Brooklyn municipal death records exist only from 1867 on, and the names of a carpenter, his wife, and his infant daughter Cecilia were as unlikely to appear in the pages of the *Brooklyn Eagle* in the 1860s as they would be in the *New York Times* today. The infant Cecilia must surely have perished; her name never turns up again. Ward's orphan "sister" Mary F. Ward, however, we shall encounter again much later; she was a talented young girl who led an obscure life as a domestic servant and remained connected with the girls' orphanage, St. Joseph's Asylum, well into her thirties, before dying of cancer on March 29, 1900. She was buried in the Holy Cross Cemetery in Brooklyn,[13] where in the spring of 1988 I located her grave.

What is significant in the turmoil of the Ward family is that as a child Thomas Ward eventually became aware—perhaps through rumor, perhaps through revealed facts—of the circumstances of his birth, and the knowledge that his father was a priest became a burden of guilt and unhappiness

that he would later carry with him to Florida. Only in his twenties (when he became a professional church musician) did he adopt the middle initial "F" and the name Francis, that of his stepfather. A good Catholic from childhood, he would never repeat his father's mistake—would not break a fundamental rule of the Church and abandon a child that he had brought into the world. He learned early on that self-discipline is the highest of values in life—the road to redemption. Thomas F. Ward was left to the mercy and generosity of the Catholic Church, which nurtured and saved him, and whatever he was to make out of his life, he would not betray his bond to the Church.

How did the Catholic Church and the Sisters of St. Joseph save Thomas F. Ward? Where did he acquire his solid classical education and literary tastes, suggested by his gift of the Byron volume to Delius? The clue appears in the following extract from the *Catholic Review*, an obscure Brooklyn periodical. Of a meeting of the St. John's Alumni Association assembled near Fort Greene Park on September 2, 1878, the paper informs us that: "At the club rooms of Mr. Theodore, on Carleton Ave . . . Mr. Thomas Ward . . . arose and expressed his delight at meeting his old friends under such happy circumstances, and amidst great cheering proposed a toast to Father Landry, the well-known president of St. John's in its early days" (September 14, 1878).

With dozens of other "Thomas Wards" to investigate in Brooklyn's city directories, weeks passed before I bothered to pursue such an unpromising lead. The article seemed to describe the salutations of an old man, not the toast of a twenty-two-year-old graduate. Ward, however, eventually proved to be not only the spontaneous speaker at the reunion but, it turned out, a member of the first class of St. John's College, which had opened its doors in September 1870 to a class of forty-seven young scholars, a student body that rapidly expanded to 140 by the end of the first term.[14] The College Hall, where the first classes were held, still stands as part of St. John the Baptist Church at the corner of Willoughby and Lewis Avenues in the Bedford-Stuyvesant district; it would not have been a very long walk for Ward from the orphanage in adjoining Crown Heights.

Surviving commencement records show that the fourteen-year-old Ward was a brilliant student from the start. At the first commencement exercises in June 1871, he took seven awards, including second prizes for writing and Christian doctrine and a first in Latin. The Latin prize was mentioned in the *Brooklyn Daily Union* on June 27, 1871, as was the strong Catholic indoctrina-

The building of the original St. John's College, corner of Willoughby and Lewis Avenues. (Photo by Robert Beckhard.)

tion of St. John's educational program and its optimistic outlook on America's future, an ideology that doubtless influenced Ward's philosophy and moral character:

> There can be no reasonable doubt that [St. John's College] will win its way in a very short time to eminence among the educational houses of Brooklyn, nay, rival the most prominent of them. . . . The educational tone is just what it should be: It has the true ring of Americanism, all nationalities but one are forgotten, and fealty to that is inculcated in every line written or read. America, their country, the noblest and the best, is held up to the juvenile, and endeared to him by the daily lessons taught in this admirable institute.

In 1872, the St. John's Literary Union, the first student organization of the new college, was founded, with Thomas Ward of "Albany and Wyckoff Street[s]" (i.e., St. John's Home) elected as its corresponding secretary.[15] The Literary Union aspired to lofty, idealistic goals. Sponsored by Rev. J. T. Landry, president of the college, it aimed "to foster the love of literature in the minds of its members, to form a close bond of friendship between them, and to enable them to speak with ease, grace and propriety, when the occasion requires it." Its motto was *Veritas semper vincit* (Truth always conquers).[16] Of a February 24, 1873, meeting of that organization (with Mayor Powell and "the elite of Brooklyn Society" among the spectators), the *Brooklyn Eagle* reported the following day that a lively debate took place on the subject "Has the 19th Century Produced Greater Men of Genius than Any Other?" Ward and a colleague presented the case for the affirmative. The result? According to the paper, "The advocates of the 19th century men, having only a little more than half a century to find their great men, and their opponents having

Left: The college classrooms of Thomas Ward. (Photo by Robert Beckhard.)
Below: Program of the St. John's Literary Union, June 24, 1872. (Archives of St. John's University.)

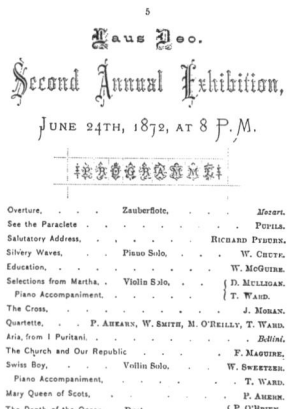

St. John's Literary Union.

The object of this Society is to foster the love of Literature in the minds of its members; to form a close bond of friendship between them; and to enable them to speak with ease, grace and propriety, when the occasion requires it.

ITS MOTTO IS:

" Veritas Semper Vincit."

OFFICERS:

President, ... PHILIP AHEARN.
Vice-President, . . . THOMAS CARROLL.
Rec. Secretary, . . . LUKE GRACE.
Cor. Secretary, . . . THOMAS WARD.
Treasurer, ... MICHAEL O'REILLY.
Critic, ... JAMES COSTELLO.
Sergeant-at-Arms, . . JOSEPH LOWREY.

Laus Deo.

Second Annual Exhibition,

JUNE 24TH, 1872, AT 8 P.M.

Overture, . . . Zauberflote, . . .	*Mozart.*
See the Paraclete	PUPILS.
Salutatory Address, ...	RICHARD PYBURN.
Silvery Waves, . . Piano Solo, . . .	W. CHUTE.
Education, ...	W. McGUIRE.
Selections from Martha, . Violin Solo, . . {	D. MULLIGAN.
Piano Accompaniment, ... {	T. WARD.
The Cross, ...	J. MORAN.
Quartette, . . P. AHEARN, W. SMITH, M. O'REILLY, T. WARD.	
Aria, from I Puritani, ...	*Bellini.*
The Church and Our Republic	F. MAGUIRE.
Swiss Boy, . . . Violin Solo, . . .	W. SWEETZER.
Piano Accompaniment, ...	T. WARD.
Mary Queen of Scots, ...	P. AHEARN.
The Depth of the Ocean, . Duet, . . {	P. O'BRIEN.
{	W. TIERNEY.
Civilization, ...	A. KAVANAGH.
Pot Pourri, from Freischutz . .	*Weber.*
Morals of Ancient and Modern Times, .	W. DURACK.

Award of Medals and Premiums.

The St. John's Literary Union, ca. 1872. (Queensborough Public Library.)

the history of eighteen centuries to ransack for brilliant examples, got worsted, and the decision of the judges was against them."

When I visited the former college in January 1987, I found that the classrooms where Thomas Ward had won his academic awards had miraculously escaped the many renovations made in the old building. The kindly priest of St. John the Baptist, Father Stephen Strouse, led me from one ghostly, abandoned room to another as he reminisced about the school's days of glory in Brooklyn, decades before St. John's became a large university and moved to Queens.

In a blurred photograph of the St. John's Literary Union, which had met near these very rooms, twenty young men in formal dress and a priest (Rev. Landry?) gaze out. One of them must be Thomas F. Ward. Perhaps it is the seven officers of the society who are seated on the front row with the priest; Ward might be one of this smaller group.

On October 6, 1989, two agents of the Federal Bureau of Investigation's (FBI) New York office compared a greatly enlarged copy of this photograph with a much later verified photograph of Ward and offered a professional, if inconclusive, forensic guess with which I concur: Ward is the third person from the right side on the second row. Except for this sphinx-like portrait, the original of which has disappeared from the St. John's University Archives, no other photograph of Ward during his Brooklyn days has survived.

The romantic literary tastes of youth instilled in Ward at that time—the love of Byron's poetry, for instance—would surely have remained with him in Florida. Perhaps it is not presumptuous to believe that some of Frederick Delius's love of American literature (for Longfellow, Whitman, Mark Twain) had its origins at the corner of Willoughby and Lewis Streets in Brooklyn.

Whitman, who became Delius's favorite American poet and the inspiration of some of his greatest works, was a very real presence in the Brooklyn of Ward's day. On March 24, 1877, the *Eagle* notes that the poet had "visited Brooklyn this morning for the first time in many years, and took occasion to stroll up to Fort Greene, the City Hall, and the old and now busy thoroughfares so familiar to him in other days" and that though "mentally alert, . . . physically, age and disease have told upon him."

Ward, at age seventeen, graduated from St. John's College on June 24, 1873, taking honors among the 158 students in his class in seven categories: French, natural philosophy, declamation, Livy and Arnold, algebra, trigonometry, and bookkeeping, the latter three revealing the practical side of his nature.[17] On this date he played a piano solo, "La Danse des Fées," a showy, sentimental piece by the French composer and piano virtuoso Alfred Jaëll (1832–82); the next morning's *Daily Times* found the performance "a beautiful solo and well executed," bringing "hearty applause." On the occasion of the literary debate at the Literary Union four months before, Ward had performed a similar work, "Les Fleurs des Alpes," op. 165, by the Austrian pianist Jules Egghard (1834–67), a piece whose repeated arpeggios and flashy chromatic runs (which, however, lead to numerous musical dead ends) was "much admired" by the audience, according to the *Daily Times* of February 25, 1873. Apart from these references, little is known about Ward's music-making during this period.

In a few surviving programs and newspaper notices, we find him accompanying colleagues at commencement exercises—in June 1872, for example, in the anonymous "Swiss Boy," with his classmate "W. Sweetzer," and "Selections from Martha," with "D. Mulligan," another violinist-colleague— and, at the orphans' Christmas benefit on December 21, 1876, conducting the vocal "Yankee Minute Men" and accompanying "Take This Letter to My Mother" and "Mother's Prayer," surely tearjerkers and no doubt heartrendingly presented. The *Catholic Review* reported on New Year's Day 1877 that the Christmas entertainment had been organized "for the purpose of providing the poor children of the parish with books."

The evidence is strong that the young Ward had a fondness for vernacular music, embraced it openly, and perhaps communicated this openness to his pupil Delius later in Florida, for the young Englishman from a cultivated family of German origin accepted American vernacular music readily and did not hesitate to incorporate it into his own compositions. The recurring

nostalgia in Delius's later music could certainly have found roots in nine-teenth-century America, where preoccupation with the past was a strong theme in sentimental and patriotic popular music such as the songs mentioned above. What can be more nostalgic than the "silent backward tracings" (to quote Whitman in Delius's *Songs of Farewell*) of an orphan toward his or her mother—a theme of many popular ballads of the day?

Moreover, concerts by "colored singers" from the South, including songs of the sort that influenced Delius's *Appalachia,* were not uncommon in the Brooklyn of Ward's time. For example, the Hampton Colored Singers of Virginia performed there in April 1873, and the Virginia Jubilee Singers presented "Slave Songs of the South" in May 1876.[18] Ward could have heard such groups, and we cannot rule out the possibility of his influence on Delius in this area of experience.

But that is only one aspect of Ward's musical world. Concerning his serious music, the *Daily Times* on April 15, 1873, provided the following astonishing report about the musical ability of the seventeen-year-old orphan, playing at an entertainment given at St. John's Home: "The piano duets, solos and accompaniments were excellent, especially Master Ward's. This young gentleman is a piano prodigy, although he never has taken a lesson. He performed several pieces with wonderful ease and precision." Regrettably, the critic fails to identify composers and compositions in Ward's repertoire.

It is known that at the college Rev. Landry was an excellent choir director and conducted the St. John's chorus with "a precision that could only have been attained by diligent rehearsal."[19] There is no proof, however, that Ward studied with him. Nor is there any evidence that the Sisters of St. Joseph taught the boy the rudiments of music. Some of the Delius literature implies that Ward studied music at the Leipzig Conservatory (and hence urged his student Delius to follow in his tracks), but a recent search through the old records of the Conservatory completely rules out this possibility.[20]

For the answer to the mystery of where Ward received enough composition technique to influence Delius for a lifetime, we must return to Mrs. Richmond's "Rosetta stone" letter and the "Prof. Lorentz" whom she mentions twice. This letter and other circumstantial evidence suggest that, after graduation from St. John's College in 1873, Ward studied with one of the most colorful musicians of nineteenth-century Brooklyn, the composer, organist, and man-about-town John M. Loretz Jr.

John M. Loretz during the Civil War. (Music Division, New York Public Library at Lincoln Center.)

John Loretz's name appears frequently in the Brooklyn press during the period Ward lived in the city. He was usually characterized as the "celebrated" or "brilliant" organist. "A famous teacher of that time" (to use Mrs. Richmond's phrase) but completely forgotten today, Loretz can be found in only one book about nineteenth-century American music, Rupert Hughes's *Contemporary American Composers*, where he is described as a "veteran composer" of sacred music and comic operas who by 1900 had "passed his opus 200."[21]

Born in Lorraine in 1840 but brought up in Brooklyn, Loretz went to Paris to study music with his uncle, the well-known organist Alexandre Guilmant (1837–1911).[22] Upon his return to Brooklyn, Loretz assumed the musical directorship of the Park Theatre and afterwards, during a long and distinguished career, he held posts at a number of local churches, both Catholic and Protestant, including St. Ann's, the Church of the Sacred Heart, St. Peter's, and St. Agnes's. He possessed an enormous ego and his escapades frequently made him the center of local controversy. He enjoyed improvising publicly in the styles of the great composers, and he had one of his grand masses bound in morocco (at a personal expense of three hundred dollars) to send to Pope Pius IX.[23] His escalating marital problems and turbulent divorce trial became front-page news in 1874–75. The *Eagle* avidly pursued the scandal, as the following headlines illustrate:

February 2, 1874: "She Accuses Him of Tampering with Her Bank Account"

February 13, 1875: "She Accuses Him of Being Cruel and Inhuman—He Accuses Her of Being Vain, Heartless, Extravagant and Under the Influence of His Mother-In-Law"

February 19, 1875: "She Accuses Her Husband of Cruelty and Abandonment and of Circulating Atrocious and Malicious Falsehoods Respecting to Her—She Says He Won't Deliver Up Her Wedding Presents, and Is About to Quit the Country"

Almost twenty years after his marital turmoil, the *Eagle* reported on June 29, 1893, that the professor had been fired from his job at St. Agnes for visiting a pub across the street from the church—during the pastor's sermon. According to one Brooklyn priest with whom I spoke, Loretz's behavior was a clear indicator of the quality of the sermons of that time!

Loretz was famous locally as an organ virtuoso. Of an "improvised symphony," *Music of Nature*, performed at the Church of the Sacred Heart in 1876 (about the time Ward could have been studying with him), the *Catholic Review* wrote:

> [One heard] the gathering of clouds, the thunder's peal, the hiss of the lightning, the crash of the thunderbolt, the frightened cry of the terror-stricken animals, while through and above all the steady splash of the rain-pour was vividly realized. In fact so thorough and natural was the imitation that one of the ushers, fearing that those in the neighborhood of the windows would get wet, tugged at the window cords until, in the audible smiles of those near him, he discovered how ridiculous he was making himself. (September 30, 1876)

His compositions were widely performed and published, and one opera, *The Pearl of Bagdad*, was a huge local hit when produced in 1872 at the Brooklyn Lyceum.[24] As a U.S. Navy Bandmaster during the Civil War, he composed three "American Anthems on the Triumph of Liberty and Union over Slavery and Treason" (1865) for chorus and piano, all celebrating the raising of the American flag over Fort Sumter.

Despite his affectation of modesty, Loretz was apparently a tireless propagandist for his own music, an artist with some awareness of the isolation of the American composer. Writing to the well-known diva Emma Thursby

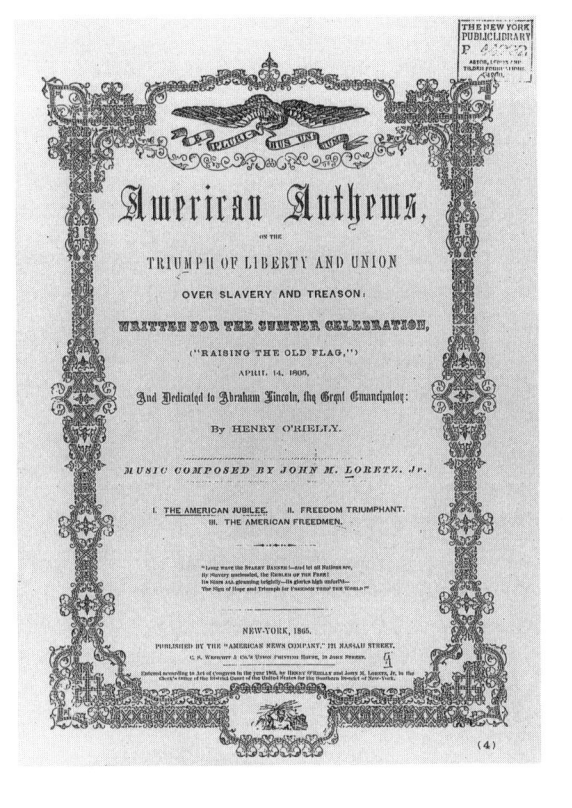

John M. Loretz, "American Anthems" (1865). Title page. (Music Division, New York Public Library at Lincoln Center.)

(1845–1931) to urge her to perform one of his vocal solos, he made a special plea for the American composer—and revealed his own roguish sense of humor:

My Dear Lady,

Pardon me for taking the liberty of addressing you but I noticed in the American Art Journal that you are going to sing works of American authors. Would you sing one of my Ave Marias? If you will I will forward it to you with a few others that you may chirp.

There is a general feeling that American or resident composers are not able to write music. Now if you think well of it I will send you an Ave Maria that was composed at Flushing when you were a pupil in that school, and . . . a Polonaise in which you can warble to your heart's content. It is new and has never been sung by any singer and is still in manuscript. I have had pretty hard luck to get music forward because I have been bashful about it but I gathered courage and thought I would ask you now—

since my last work the Sacred Heart Mass has met with such success in France. Hoping I will receive an answer from you and wishing you every good thing,

Respectfully,

John M. Loretz, Jr.[25]

It is probable that Loretz met with many rejections. He later declared Brooklyn "dead to real music" and threatened to move to Mexico because of Brooklyn's lack of appreciation for men of genius like himself, a situation dramatically reported by the *Eagle* on October 16, 1904, under the headline "Composer to Go to Mexico at 56." Loretz characteristically misstated his age, which was actually sixty-four in 1904, a fact confirmed by census records.[26] Shortly thereafter, in 1905, he did move, but to the unknown village of Hollywood, California, where he resumed his career as an organist.[27] He died of a cerebral hemorrhage in 1912.[28] Loretz's Brooklyn residences at 159 Adelphi Street and 185 Washington Avenue, where he received his students, still stand today, giving mute testimony to a colorful musical era.

John M. Loretz, undated photograph from the *Brooklyn Daily Eagle*, December 30, 1931 (Long Island University, Brooklyn). (Photo by Jan Coward.)

What threads connect Ward to Loretz? First, there was no other music teacher named "Lorentz" active in Brooklyn and Long Island during this period. (To Mrs. Richmond, the unconventional French name "Loretz" would have sounded like the more common German one "Lorentz.") A second clue is the piano piece "Les Fleurs des Alpes": just three weeks before Ward performed it at St. John's College in February 1873, it had been played at a benefit concert featuring "the celebrated organist" Loretz and his music, the pianist on this occasion being "Mrs. Everett," probably a pupil of Loretz.[29] Perhaps this was a favorite teaching piece of Loretz, played by many of his students—including Ward.

It was probably during the period 1874–76 that Ward studied with Loretz—a period of Ward's life that is scantily documented. In 1873 he is described as an eighteen-year-old "musician" on the staff of the Catholic orphanage, which at that time housed 419 orphans, ages two to sixteen.[30] It seems very probable that during this time he was able to receive an intensive course in theory and composition from Loretz, acquiring enough technique by Easter Sunday 1876 to assume a position as organist and choirmaster of the Church of the Assumption in downtown Brooklyn.

The timing of Ward's first professional post suggests a further possible connection to Loretz. Just two weeks before that Easter Sunday, April 16, 1876, when Ward surfaces at this church, an advertisement had run in the Brooklyn Eagle on April 1 and 3:

> Wanted [by] an organist (Student of Loretz Jr.). Desires a position from May 1, a Church with congregational singing preferred. Terms very low. (Contact 325 Carleton Ave.)

Could the job-seeker have been Thomas F. Ward? The address "325 Carleton Ave." yields no clues in the census, but perhaps it is connected with the "club rooms of Mr. Theodore on Carleton Ave." in which Ward was to toast Father Landry just two years later.

On January 1, 1877, the twenty-year-old Ward was judged by the Catholic Review as "a young gentleman of fine execution on the piano, who bids fair to take an enviable position in his profession" and as one who conducted vocal music "very ably." The Eagle, reviewing a benefit for St. John's Home, described him on June 8, 1877, as "an accomplished and skillful musician, who was formerly an inmate of the institution." He had been able after 1875 to move out of the orphanage to rooms at 66 Fifth Avenue, just off Flatbush

Thomas F. Ward's residence at 66 Fifth Avenue, Brooklyn. (Photo by Robert Beckhard.)

Avenue, where the 1880 census and Brooklyn directories of 1882 and 1883 list him as "music teacher." (This, his only known Brooklyn residence, on the edge of Park Slope, still survives in a neighborhood of rapid gentrification.)

As typical examples of the repertoire that Ward seems to have preferred, we might single out two piano pieces, "La Danse des Fées" by Alfred Jaëll (Ward's pianistic triumph at St. John's College) and John Loretz's polka "The Gay Old Time" (1860), the latter dedicated "to the Jolly six," doubtless drinking companions of the extroverted professor.

Both of these works—the first by a French friend of Louis Moreau Gottschalk and the second by a twenty-year-old Brooklynite—are typical of the salon tradition reflected in American parlors of the mid-nineteenth century. Sentimental meditations, polkas, galops, waltzes, and especially variations on popular tunes and opera arias—usually played with virtuosic flair—were much in vogue and accepted as cultivated art music at that time. It would be wrong to cast condescending cultural judgment on the music, or even to attempt to place it unfavorably opposite the great European romantic tradition. This music, with its unabashed emotionalism, could be immediately appealing to Americans aspiring to high culture. The compositions of Richard Hoffman, George William Warren, William Mason, and especially the American composer without parallel, Louis Moreau Gottschalk—all men had strong ties to Brooklyn—reflect accurately the optimistic American temperament of that time. It is music which the Gottschalk scholar Robert Offergeld has aptly called "the music of democratic sociability."[31] It was anathema to cultural arbiters, such as John Sullivan Dwight (of *Dwight's Journal*), who preferred their Mendelssohn and Schumann, but it attracted a vast American audience nevertheless. At its best, it was not "stiff and labored" but had

Alfred Jaëll, "La Danse des Fées." Jaëll (b. Trieste 1832–d. Paris 1882) was known as "le pianiste voyageur" and traveled in the United States in 1852–54. He was a friend of Gottschalk, who dedicated his "La Moissonneuse" (1849) to him. (Library of Congress.)

John M. Loretz, "The Gay Old Time, Polka" (1860). (Music Division, New York Public Library at Lincoln Center.)

"melody, spontaneity, and naïveté," qualities that Gottschalk, as William Mason relates, found conspicuously lacking in, for instance, Schumann.[32] It is significant that Loretz himself performed Gottschalk's music on occasion, at a time when it was already beginning to go out of fashion. The *Eagle* noted on November 26, 1879, for example, that the ever popular Loretz and "Miss Boyle" performed Gottschalk's *La Gallina*, op. 53, "in a style which again roused the enthusiasm of the audience."

Not only Ward's contrapuntal training but also his experience in the sentimental cultured tradition influenced Delius later at Solano Grove. Delius's first attempts at composition in 1885 in Florida, the Loretz-like polka entitled "Zum Carnival"—published in Jacksonville—and the parlor piano piece "Pensées mélodieuses," a near relative of Jaëll's piece, accurately reflect this aspect of Ward's Brooklyn tastes, a combination of sheer exuberance and unashamed sentimentality.

Frederick Delius, "Zum Carnival" (1885). (By permission of Boosey & Hawkes, Ltd.)

Having established himself in 1876 as a professional musician with a secure post at the Church of the Assumption, how did Ward spend the remaining eight years of his Brooklyn period? Astonishingly, he seems never to have taken an active part in the daily professional musical life of Brooklyn. No evidence exists of even a single involvement by Ward in a concert unrelated to the Catholic Church. Two reasons might account for this extraordinary silence on the part of an individual whose gifts were so promising.

First, by 1875 Ward's responsibilities at the large orphanage must have taken a great deal of his time. For instance, the *Catholic Review* reports on July 29, 1876, that the teaching of the orphans at St. John's Home—now numbering 680—was entrusted to only seven persons. Church-related functions (performances, benefits, charities, sodalities) may have precluded secular concert activities. Typical of the church-related concerts in which Ward participated, most of which escaped the press's notice, was "a grand Musical

and Dramatic Entertainment" given at the Brooklyn Athenaeum to aid the Christian Brothers in their upkeep of St. James's pro-Cathedral School on Jay Street, the site of Ward's first orphanage residence. All we know about this program of February 2, 1881, which included various glees and vocal solos, was that it "gave entire satisfaction" and "the accompaniments, by Prof. Ward, were in keeping with the rest of the programme."[33]

Second, and foremost, Ward was an industrious and dedicated Brooklyn church musician. At the Church of the Assumption, he assumed his first professional post, from 1876 to 1878, under the popular but demanding Rev. William Keegan, pastor of the church since 1852. There is a possibility that Ward's connection with this church was already established by 1874, when he was eighteen years old. The *Catholic Review* of April 18, 1874, reports that on Easter of that year Father Keegan was the celebrant for the solemn high mass, in which "Mr. Ward" served as "master of ceremonies"—that is, as the principal altar boy. Founded in 1842, the original church building at the corner of York and Jay Streets was demolished in 1903 to make room for the runway onto the Manhattan Bridge, then under construction, and the congregation removed to its present location on Cranberry Street in Brooklyn Heights.

In comparison with the other large Catholic churches in Brooklyn, the Assumption does not seem to have played a major role in the city's musical life. Of note, however, is that in his first Easter service in 1876, Ward presented Haydn's Sixteenth Mass (Hob. XXII:12) and Mozart's Twelfth Mass (K. 246a) with a "very efficient choir," the *Eagle* reported on April 18. Covering the Silver Jubilee (twenty-fifth anniversary) of Father Keegan's ordination, the religious press noted the performance (in the presence of Bishop Laughlin and the mayor of Brooklyn) of Mozart's "Gloria" (from the "12th Mass") with Ward "officiating at the organ, and a full choir assisting."[34]

Delivering the address in honor of Father Keegan on that day was one of the most illustrious churchmen of nineteenth-century Brooklyn, Rev. Sylvester Malone (1821–1899), founder and pastor of the great church of SS. Peter and Paul in Williamsburg. A famous orator and a man of liberal views on a variety of civic subjects, Father Malone must have been impressed with Ward's music-making, for by Thanksgiving 1878, only a few weeks later, he had hired the young man for his own church. Of Ward's earliest documented performance at SS. Peter and Paul, the *Daily Times* reported on November 29 that the building was "filled with devout worshippers at each [mass]. The

Left: The Old Church of the Assumption, amid construction of the Manhattan Bridge. (Brooklyn Historical Society.) Right: Rev. Sylvester Malone, photo from *The Golden Jubilee of the Rev. Sylvester Malone* (1895). (Brooklyn Historical Society.)

very excellent music was rendered by a powerful choir under the leadership of the new organist, Mr. Thomas Ward."

The high quality of music at Father Malone's church during the five and a half years of Ward's tenure is well documented in the press. Established in 1844, the church had been built by the most famous architect of Catholic Churches in America, Patrick C. Keely. Its 150-foot spire dominated the Brooklyn waterfront (from which it was only one block removed) and, after the reconstruction of the church's interior in 1878 just prior to Ward's arrival, its magnificent stained glass windows, depicting the stations of the cross, were the glory of Williamsburg. One of the largest and most impressive churches in the Diocese of Brooklyn, it could accommodate up to two thousand people on festive occasions.[35] (Regrettably, the stately building was demolished in 1958, after a long period of deterioration.)

At SS. Peter and Paul, Ward presented masses by Haydn, Mozart, and Beethoven, and religious works of Mendelssohn and Gounod, in addition to everyday Catholic service music by now-forgotten composers such as F. J. Heinrich Wiegand (1842–99), Paolo Giorza (1832–1914), Vincent Novello (1781–1861), and Johann Wenzel Kalliwoda (1801–66). A typical *Daily Times* report from this period, for SS. Peter and Paul's Day 1879, reads: "The music which was under the direction of the organist Mr. F. F. Ward [sic], and an

SS. Peter and Paul's Church, Williamsburg, photo from *The Golden Jubilee of the Rev. Sylvester Malone* (1895). (Brooklyn Historical Society.)

efficient orchestra, was unusually excellent. The overture was from 'La Muette de Portici,' by Auber, while at the Offertory Miss Spieker & Mr. Phinsky sang Verdi's 'O Salutaris' as a duet. The Mass which was sung was Haydn's Third [Nelson Mass?]" (June 30, 1879). At Easter 1882, the newspaper provided this generous coverage of the service:

> Rev. Father Ward preached at the High Mass at Sts. Peter and Paul's Church, Father Gallagher celebrating. The sermon was on the lesson of the day and was of an eloquent character. The decorations were very fine, the congregation was large—so were the collections—and the music was fine. Haydn's Fourth Mass [Hob. XXII: 13] was sung and Giorza's Regina Caeli at the offertory. Credit is due, as far as the music was concerned, to Professor Ward and his quartette, Mme. M. Bonligny, Miss Adelina Richards, Mr. W. H. Smith and Mr. Ernest Koko. (April 10, 1882)

(It should be noted that "Rev. Father [Hugh B.] Ward," Father Malone's assistant at SS. Peter and Paul, was not related to Thomas F. Ward.)

Despite such good reviews, Ward soon found that a church position alone could not provide a livelihood. On May 1, 1879, the *Eagle*, underlining the grim economic realities for church musicians ("Songsters"), observed that the rigid local economy had forced a cutback in the expenses of choirs and

that organists in particular had suffered considerably, their salaries being far below what they had been. The term "Professor Ward," which appears around this time, is evidence that he had begun to teach privately to make ends meet.

Fortunately, musicians could find many ways to supplement their incomes. An obscure newspaper item reveals that in the summer of 1880 Ward was an instructor in music and gymnastics at the School of the Holy Cross, an institution administered by the Sisters of St. Joseph and located then, as now, at 35 Snyder Avenue in Flatbush. On July 1 the *Eagle* mentioned that he also provided music for the school's commencement services, held on June 29 in the nearby Flatbush Town Hall, now a historical landmark only recently saved from demolition. We can presume that he would have been connected to other such church academies during his Brooklyn years. The Sisters of St. Joseph had also been associated closely with the SS. Peter and Paul's Church since 1856, and Father Malone helped them establish St. Joseph's Academy (1857) opposite the church,[36] but it cannot be verified that Ward taught there, since documents of the Catholic Church academies of that period either have been lost or, as one Church official told me, are "floating around," their exact locations unknown to anyone.[37]

Aside from notices of Ward's teaching and performing, what about composing? Brooklyn newspapers provide some documentation that Ward was indeed a composer. We can safely assume that he would have written (or improvised) many of his church's anonymous "preludes, overtures, postludes" faithfully listed in the newspapers during the Easter and Christmas seasons. The earliest specific mention of Ward as a composer, however, seems to be the following account in the *Daily Times* of a "Patriotic Entertainment by the Orphan Children" of St. John's Home on George Washington's birthday in 1881: "The entertainment itself was one of the best and most interesting that the Home has ever had, and much superior to the ordinary school exercises. Professor Thomas F. Ward, a graduate of the home, was the manager and presided at the piano. . . . The programme commenced with an overture by Professor Ward, followed by a chorus by a portion of the scholars" (February 23, 1881).

Ward is mentioned more often as a composer during the early 1880s. On the feast of Saints Peter and Paul on July 2, 1882, "57 orphan boys from St. John's Home sang a mass composed by the church organist, Professor Thomas Ward, assisted by an orchestra of seven pieces," the *Eagle* reported the

The Holy Cross School in Flatbush. (Photo by Jan Coward.)

following morning. And had one attended mass at 6:00 A.M. on Christmas Day that year in Williamsburg, one would have heard Professor Ward conduct his own "Veni Creator" for the introit along with Gounod's *Messe Solennelle*, before performing the finale of Mendelssohn's First Organ Sonata as a postlude.[38]

Again, we wonder why such a talented person seems not to have mingled with or performed more often before the general public. Surely a more ominous reason for Ward's inactivity outside the Catholic Church lay in his health, in the worsening tuberculosis that would soon send him to Florida. He would not have been alone in his plight. Newspapers of the day are full of quack offers aimed at the hopeful consumptive. A typical advertisement, appearing in the *Eagle* on October 11, 1873, and presented as poetry no less, promises the invalid that consumption

Can't kill any patient who will
Take Hale's Honey of Horehound and Tar when
He's ill
Of a cough that no other prescription will
Still.

Those with tuberculosis—with the "Irish disease," as it was called—were ostracized. Around the time Ward departed from Brooklyn, the *Eagle* published an article (reprinted from the London *Pall Mall Gazette*) purporting to outline progress against the disease but offering no comfort to those who suffered from it. A Brooklynite could read therein that

[until recently] people disliked the idea of the consumptive and the healthy occupying the same bed. Nurses and others were ready with the recital of cases in which they alleged the disease had been caught from inhaling the breath of consumptive patients. And it is certainly curious to find that this old notion is at the present time receiving something which looks remarkably like confirmation at the hands of the furthest science. (May 10, 1884)

For those who could afford it, the best solution was to leave increasingly crowded Brooklyn and head South to warmer weather and open spaces.

An ardent proponent of a reconstructed—and reaccepted—South, Father Malone had made a well-publicized trip to the area (including Florida) in 1869 and had maintained contacts with the clergy there.[39] It is likely that he made it possible for Thomas Ward to move to Florida and assume a new musical post in Jacksonville in late spring 1884.

Ward's name disappears from the Brooklyn newspapers after the Easter service of April 13, 1884, and an ad that appeared in the *Eagle* on April 22–23 was probably a call for his replacement: "Wanted—organist—for a Catholic Church in Brooklyn. Address, *Eagle* office."

What lay ahead for Thomas F. Ward? Had he picked up the daily *Eagle* on January 2, 1879, he could have learned from a lengthy travelogue ("In Florida") that for the many invalids who flocked there during the winter months, along with the tourists and pleasure seekers, Jacksonville's "congenial climate is recommended by physicians to patients suffering from pulmonary complaints and other illnesses." Had he seen the same newspaper a bit more than a year later, he could have read its Jacksonville correspondent waxing exuberant over northern Florida but with a more realistic tone:

Florida is a wonderful country, one half under water. Somebody was indecent enough to say the other half ought to be, but it isn't. It is exactly on a level with the St. Johns River. One of the most remarkable features of the Peninsular State is the extraordinary climate during the Winter months. I have visited different parts of the planet we inhabit, have eaten mandarin oranges in the groves near Canton, have sucked milk from the coconuts of Java . . . sat under date palms of the Isthmus, viewed the dark-eyed señoritas of Mexico . . . but never have I found on the civilized portion of the earth, a place where a man could rise at 7 A.M., put on winter flannels and a heavy overcoat, change all this for a linen suit at 11 A.M. to 6 P.M., and resume his winter clothing at 8:00 in the evening to sit before a blazing

fire of pine logs, and sleep at night under three blankets and a spread. People with delicate lungs who propose visiting Florida may make a note of this for future reference, with my regards. (March 28, 1880)

I have quoted the correspondent's narrative extensively because, although most contemporary reports speak of Florida as a paradise in the South, this account approximated the truth: a consumptive, even if he had dreams of a comfortable and cultivated life, must not expect deliverance from his illness there—only temporary respite.

In the spring of 1884 Tom Ward and Fritz Delius arrived in the exotic southern port of Jacksonville at very nearly the same point in time, each with his own expectations: Ward in search of better health and a new future, Delius hoping to "find himself" and perhaps also to escape the pull of music and gain the acceptance of the family fold. With these two moves to the banks of the St. Johns River and Solano Grove, another chapter began in the life of Thomas Francis Ward. If Brooklyn had been his sunrise, Florida and the South would be his sunset.

✦ *Jacksonville and St. Augustine*

"Professor Ward, of course, presided at the organ."

The port of Jacksonville that confronted Thomas F. Ward in 1884 was a city of around seventeen thousand inhabitants, about equally divided between blacks and whites. It contrasted dramatically with the Brooklyn he had left. He could look out on the semitropical St. Johns River instead of the frigid East River, and rather than thoroughfares of crowded tenements he could walk sandy streets strewn with oyster shells, redolent with disagreeable odors, and lined with frame boardinghouses, each with its garden with orange trees.

In the *Brooklyn Daily Times* of February 9, 1884, shortly before Ward's arrival, an anonymous Brooklyn tourist opined that if you took away "the beautiful blue St. Johns . . . there would be but few natural charms left, [despite the] pleasant diversions at the hotels and the gay throngs that flutter up and down the broad pavements of Bay Street"; there was "a sort of little Brooklyn across a turgid stream called McCoy's Creek, a pleasant place, known like Brooklyn for its pretty girls, [but it] hardly compares with original Brooklyn any more than the wooden structure that crosses McCoy's Creek can be brought into comparison with the original Brooklyn Bridge."

Another visitor observed in the *Brooklyn Eagle* of May 8, 1881, that among the ex-Brooklynites in Jacksonville, "some men were hale and hearty, and some were pale and wan." Health-seeking refugees from the North had made many people rich—especially, he noticed, boardinghouse owners and doctors. "The number of quacks that infest Jacksonville is astonishing. . . . They come from all parts of the country with their diplomas, and their principal specialty is consumption." Describing Jacksonville as "a city made up from the sick men of the North," this reporter offered his Brooklyn readers a poignant picture of a Florida consumptive's daily life:

The weaklings . . . remain indoors till the sun comes out. . . . They are like crocodiles or alligators in this respect. They come out to get their backs warmed, and it is very sad, though laughable, to see them wandering up and down the streets, three or four at a time, and expectorating their lungs, as unconcerned as if they were merely projecting tobacco juice. The people call them "narrowbacks." . . . The visitor to almost any of the smaller hotels will find an assembly of "narrowbacks" in the waiting room. . . . They do not brood over their misfortunes, but look the world in the face and wait for the coming of the inevitable.

More optimistically, he concluded that "there is a class of invalids who only require a mild atmosphere to get them on their feet again. This class surely will find relief in Florida." From what can be detected about his daily life, at least on his arrival, Ward seems to have belonged to this more fortunate class.

Ward found rooms in a small hotel, John F. Sanford's Grand Central Boarding House, located at 14 West Monroe Street,[1] the present site of Jacksonville's Masonic Lodge. According to the *Florida State Gazetteer and Business Directory for 1883–84*, the boardinghouse was known as the "Sledge House," after its original owner, Mrs. C. A. Sledge. It was conveniently located two blocks from the Church of the Immaculate Conception, where around May of 1884 Ward assumed the post of organist and accompanist to the singers and chorus under the directorship of two prominent local musicians, Carl von Weller and Frank Ely. Unfortunately, Ward's name does not appear in the Florida state census of 1885, which would have provided, in addition to an address, many facts about him.

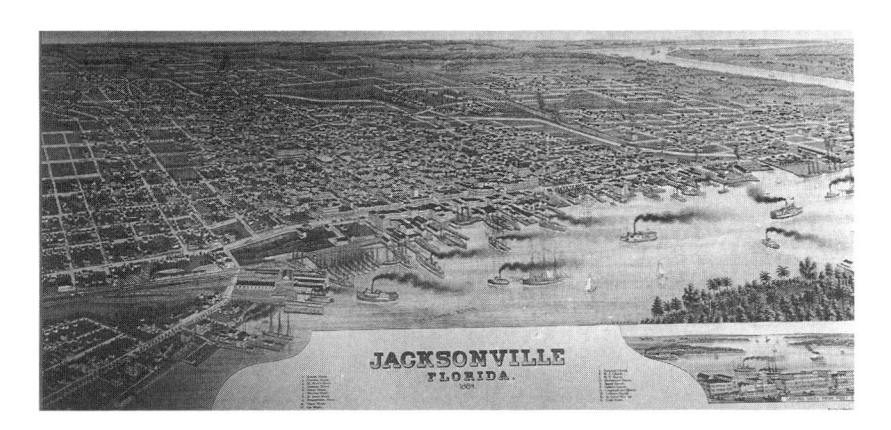

Sketch of Jacksonville, Florida, 1884. (Photo by Daryl Joseph, courtesy Richard A. Martin, Jacksonville.)

Detail of illustration on page 46. Ward's residences and the Church of the Immaculate Conception (F) are visible in upper right-hand corner.

Around 1886 (after Delius's departure from Florida), Ward moved into Mrs. Nellie L. Ward's boardinghouse at the southwest corner of Forsyth and Julia Streets, the location now occupied by one of Jacksonville's faceless sky-scrapers, the Southern Bell Tower.[2] The "Ward House" (a nice coincidence) was a three-story wooden structure accommodating twenty-five guests, "handsomely furnished throughout,"[3] and operated by a fashionable, wealthy widow, who, according to the *Jacksonville Morning News* of September 22, 1886, liked to venture each summer to the spas and "watering places" of the North. Located directly across from the Everett Hotel and the Bingham House, where in 1884 Delius had set himself up as a violin teacher, the Ward House would have been a good location from which to enter Jacksonville's social and musical milieu.

To supplement what must have been a meager income, Ward sought private students by placing an announcement in the *Florida Times-Union* of February 4 and 5, 1885, offering piano lessons at his pupils' residences, "one lesson a week, $1; two lessons, $1.75." The ad pointed out that prospective students could find him at Merryday & Paine's music store, 48 Ocean Street.

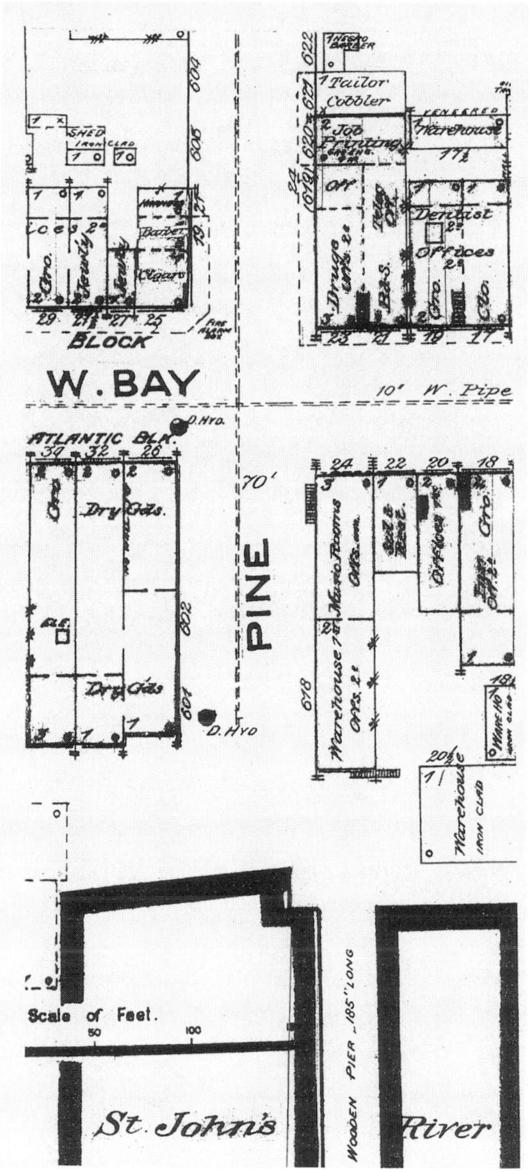

Above: Frederick Delius, 1884. (Courtesy Eric Fenby.)
Right: Meeting place of Fritz Delius and Thomas Ward at 24 West Bay Street, Jacksonville. Sanford Insurance Map of Jacksonville, 1884. (Florida Collection, Jacksonville Public Library.)

It was on a spring day in 1884 that Fritz Delius had found "Professor Ward" at the store's previous location, just off the waterfront at 24 West Bay Street,[4] and invited him to come to his orange plantation upriver and teach him the fundamentals of music composition. At this point in time Ward earned his footnote in music history.

The exotic locale for these music lessons in 1884 must have been very similar to that described by Delius thirteen years later when he revisited Solano Grove in the company of two of his bohemian Paris friends:

> I left in January for Florida and have been basking in the sunshine and enjoying this lovely place for the last three months. The climate and the flowers are extraordinary and the situation of my grove is lovely and right on the beautiful St. Johns River. . . . We have caught a young alligator about a yard long and have it in a barrel in front of the house. I am bringing a lot of snake skins back that I have killed and am sorry I cannot bring some of the flowers or a piece of the moonlight nights or some of the magnolia blossoms and orange blossoms. The sunsets here are something remarkable and always different varying between the most delicate colours on some nights to the most lurid and ferocious hues on others. The scenery is lovely and I should say remarkably well adapted for a painter. There is a nice little house on the place with a broad verandah facing the St. Johns River and standing in the middle of the orange trees. In front of the house is a garden with gardenias, hibiscus and a few other tropical flowers of which I do not know the names. Over the veranda an enormous honeysuckle creeps and in front of the house to the right and near the river an enormous live oak stands and shades a sort of lawn of very green grass. We have had the most delicious weather all the time and I have enjoyed my stay immensely.[5]

The writer Lafcadio Hearn best captured the spiritual essence of this part of Florida. On arriving in Jacksonville, he sensed "the breath of the great St. Johns River, sweetened by mingling with the mightier breath of the sea, and bearing with it scent of orange flowers and odors of magnolia." Sailing past Solano Grove at around the period that Delius and Ward were there, Hearn confided to his journal aboard the steamship *Osceola* bound for Palatka:

> Blue miles of water to right and left; the azure enormity ever broadening and brightening before. Viewing the majesty of the flood, the immortal beauty of the domed forests crowning its banks, the day-magic of colors shifting and interblending through leagues of light, a sense of inexpressible reverence fills the mind of the observer,—a sense of the divinity of Nature, the holiness of beauty.
>
> These are the visions we must call celestial; this is the loveliness that is sacred, that is infinite,—the poetry of heaven.[6]

We can imagine that Ward, coming up frequently by river steamer, knew this scene well. He would also have known Albert A. Anderson, Delius's twenty-one-year-old black caretaker, and Albert's thirteen-year-old wife-to-be Eliza B. Sanks, both children of former slaves, who lived on "Solano Neck," as the huge bend in the river was called. Ward occasionally would have seen Eliza's younger sister Julia, who helped with the chores. Surely he also heard the old slave songs they and their friends sang for Delius.

One of the songs the Andersons sang must have been the melody that became Delius's text for the final choral variation of *Appalachia*:

> After night has gone comes the day,
> The dark shadows will fade away,
> T'ords the morning lift a voice,
> Let the scented woods rejoice
> And echoes swell across the mighty stream.

Philip Heseltine described the "old folk-song" in his earliest essay about Delius's music: "It was sung to the composer by one of the negroes on his orange plantation; there were only two of them, but both appear to have been remarkably gifted. The one in question [Albert?] possessed, in addition to his extensive repertoire of folk-songs, the gift of second sight, developed to a very high pitch, while the other [Eliza?] could accomplish the astounding feat of whistling in thirds!"[7]

In 1969, when I visited Albert Anderson's elderly sister-in-law Julia Sanks in St. Augustine, in her cluttered house on McLaughlin Street in the "colored section," she recounted no vivid memories of Solano Grove like those she had colorfully imparted to Gloria Jahoda a few years before.[8] There were no tales of Delius's life in the South—of cane grindings, quail and turkey shoots, Negro spirituals and banjo picking, water moccasins and coachwhips, lady visitors, and steamships at nearby Tocoi, disembarking Yankee passengers who took the St. Johns Railway through the piney woods and palmettos to St. Augustine. She remembered little of happy times on the former orange plantation. After all, Julia Sanks was ninety-three years old in 1969, and when Delius had first lived at Solano Grove in 1884, she was an eight-year-old sharing a hard daily life with her elders. But she liked very much the tune and words of *Appalachia* when I attempted to sing them to her and, perhaps thinking back to 1897 when she was twenty-one and Delius had returned to the grove, she recalled that "Mr. Delius was a nice man; he was always at his

Delius's house at Solano Grove, 1939. (Photo by Carver Harris, Delius Collection of Martha B. Richmond, Jacksonville Public Library.)

music. Mr. Delius was a nice man. Yessir." The name of Thomas Ward, however, elicited only a blank gaze of nonrecognition. When Julia Sanks died in 1970, the last direct link to Delius, his orange plantation, and his teacher was gone.

Albert A. Anderson (1863–1925) and his wife Eliza B. Sanks Anderson (1871–1952) are buried in the old Pinehurst Cemetery in St. Augustine, their gravestones now impossible to identify. Julia Sanks (1876–1970), who never married, rests in the "Sanksville" cemetery near Picolata.

It is pointless to speculate further on the day-to-day relationship of Thomas Ward and Fritz Delius at Solano Grove. Jahoda and others have improvised on this theme, and such an attempt would be, after all, only guesswork in the absence of any documentation. Several controversial areas in this story, however, should be explored before continuing with Ward's own career, where facts can be found for a partial sketch of his life as a professional Jacksonville musician.

Just how demanding was Ward's counterpoint course? To date, Delius scholars have considered the most important document linking Ward and

Delius to be one of the composer's exercise notebooks, a volume given to the City of Jacksonville by Eric Fenby in 1968 and now located in the Swisher Library at Jacksonville University.[9] This forty-page musical sketchbook seemed to show the collaboration of student and teacher in a series of progressively more complicated harmonic and counterpoint studies. When I began this project, I too regarded the booklet's contents (basic counterpoint, harmonic modulations, fugal exercises) as offering corroboration of the thoroughness of Delius's study with Ward. Looking at the notebook more closely, however, I was puzzled by the German nomenclature (*drei-stimmige[r] Satz, enharmonische Wechslungen*, etc.), which appears even in the first pages, and by the fact that much of its content is given over to sketches for Delius's early German partsongs, pieces known to have been written after Florida. Moreover, Ward had not learned German in Brooklyn, but rather French, in which he had excelled. In the context of a teacher/pupil relationship with Delius, the German terminology made no sense. In 1989, after further study, I concluded that the "Jacksonville Notebook" has nothing to do with Ward—at least not directly.

The notebook (on page six) seems to give the date "1887" after a word that to my untrained eye appears to be "Leipzig." Lionel Carley, archivist of the Delius Trust, has also read the date as "1887" and interpreted the preceding word as possibly "Leipzig."[10] I received additional corroboration from the Delius Trust's adviser Robert Threlfall, who, in preparing a study of Delius's sketchbooks, doubted the exercises had originated in Florida.[11] It can now be confirmed that the notebook relates to the Leipzig Conservatory and its pedagogues, not to Jacksonville and Ward. Mislabeled many decades ago, and afterwards repeatedly mentioned in books about Delius, the sketchbook became, with the passage of time, a part of the Delius/Ward legend.[12]

But, indirectly, the notebook does suggest the thoroughness of Delius's study with Ward. In several instances, Delius simply broke off his Leipzig exercises, seemingly out of boredom. The techniques being spoon-fed to him at the Leipzig Conservatory in 1887 had already been mastered at Solano Grove three years earlier.

The circumstances of Delius's introduction to Ward are also somewhat cloudy. Was their meeting a chance encounter, an impulse on Ward's part to confront a stranger, as Heseltine suggests? In contradiction, another source alleges that Edward Suskind, a prominent Jacksonville lumberman, was responsible for the encounter. According to his obituary notice in the *Florida*

Delius Notebook, vol. 1, page 6. (Swisher Library, Jacksonville University.)

Times-Union of January 13, 1931, the Stuttgart-born Suskind, whose home was a gathering place for Jacksonville's music lovers, befriended Delius and located a teacher for him: "the organist of one of Jacksonville's churches." It seems likely that Suskind's memory was faulty after the passage of nearly half a century, for Delius's own account (via Heseltine) has an immediacy that cannot be denied. A meeting of Ward and Delius was almost certain to happen, however, given the fact that Ward's teaching brought him daily to Merryday & Paine's. Only the law of probability detracts from the romance of the well-known story. [13]

Delius's piano, Delius Museum, Jacksonville University. (Photo by Daryl Joseph.)

How much time did Ward actually spend with Delius at Solano Grove? William Randel suggests in his authoritative essay about Delius's American years that Ward's stay was brief.[14] In one sense, it is irrelevant whether he spent six months teaching Delius on the river (as Heseltine and Fenby relate) or whether, in view of his Jacksonville responsibilities, he stayed for a shorter time (as Randel suggests). The essence of the experience remains the same: Delius's spiritual revelation in idyllic physical surroundings and steady musical progress under the guidance of a strong intellect and sympathetic comrade.

One event, however, seems to tilt the story conclusively toward the longer stay. Delius's piano from Solano Grove resides today in the Delius House Museum on the campus of Jacksonville University. The square grand piano, manufactured by Hazelton Brothers of New York, is only one of the artifacts in the Delius House, which was disassembled, transported in 1961 to Jacksonville University, and then renovated. Away from the swamps and wildlife of Solano Grove, the cottage, a shrine of Deliana, now sits forlornly between a track field and an air-conditioning plant.

Beneath the piano's soundboard is a mysterious inscription: "Del F Delius Solano Grove Wait Thom Ward." The message indicates that Ward arranged delivery ("Del") of the piano to Delius's river home ("F Delius Solano Grove")

just after it was purchased ("Wait Thom Ward"). It suggests strongly that upon meeting Ward, Delius quickly made the decision to study with him.

In 1961, Ken Lueck of Daytona Beach found the Delius piano in a storage warehouse in that city, where it had lain abandoned. Purchasing the piano for his daughter, Lueck later discovered the inscription and asked a Florida musicologist, Charles Hofmann, to decipher it. The piano was taken to the Delius Museum in 1965.[15]

For years, both the existence of Ward's message and the authenticity of the piano have been suspect. Gloria Jahoda states adamantly that an elderly black man told her that "squatters cut it up for firewood and sold the keys for ivory"![16]

On July 8, 1991, I rediscovered the faded inscription and, after speaking with Ken Lueck's widow in Daytona Beach soon thereafter, abandoned my own reservations about its authenticity. The piano now in Jacksonville is the instrument at which Delius and Ward worked in 1884–85 and on which Delius composed most of his Piano Concerto in 1897.

I see little reason to question that Delius, Ward, and the newly purchased piano all soon steamed to the orange plantation, as Heseltine colorfully relates. It should be noted too that Ward's advertisement for students did not appear in the *Times-Union* until February 1885, more than nine months after his arrival in the South, suggesting that until early 1885 he had no time for private pupils, the challenge of teaching Delius being his most important

Ward's inscription on Delius's piano, Delius Museum, Jacksonville University. (Photo by Robert Beckhard.)

concern. Finally, Ward's absence during 1884–85 from local newspaper re-
portage of Jacksonville's concert life implies that much of his time was spent
elsewhere.

We should also consider the sheer expense for Ward of traveling frequently
by boat to Solano Grove (the Picolata landing) from Jacksonville. Many years
later Bartola Genovar, a native of St. Augustine, gave a colorful account of
this journey. The stagecoach from St. Augustine to Picolata "cost the traveler
$2, and the steamboat fare to Jacksonville was $3," Genovar remembered.
"Time elapsed from St. Augustine was anywhere from seven to nine hours
by the coach and boat route."[17]

Finally, not until March 3, 1885, does Ward's name appear in a music
review, when he is listed in the *Times-Union* as the performer of an anonymous "piano solo" for a fire benefit concert at the Park Theatre. Surely, had
he been active in the city, he would not have needed the greater part of a
year to establish his musical credentials.

Ward's church responsibilities could not have taken much of his time either, even from the outset. Like most of the South, Jacksonville was full of
anti-Catholic sentiment, and the Catholic Church, established in the city in
1860, concerned itself with doctrine and its struggle to survive, not with
the ornamental function of music. Apart from the Easter and Christmas feasts,
music was subservient to the daily ritual of the mass, where plainchant suf-
ficed, a practice confirmed by the *Times-Union*'s comment on Christmas Day
1886 that "Solemn High Mass is seldom celebrated in this city."

Finally, in the area of controversy, what should we make of the whis-
pered-about pleasures of Solano Grove that have attracted the attention of
writers about Delius? Whether he had a black mistress, as he told Percy
Grainger,[18] or was amorously involved with his Picolata neighbor, the musically gifted Jutta Bell-Ranske (more likely), Delius's sex life in Florida has
remained a mystery. What were the extra-musical pleasures that Delius and
Ward shared together—aside from an occasional alligator or rattlesnake shoot?
Two men occupying a house in the wilderness for six months, as Randel
points out, would be "sure to raise a few eyebrows."[19] A few devotees of
Delius's music have suggested that the two had a homosexual relationship,
but I have uncovered nothing in Ward's character that suggests that possibility. Nor do the facts of Delius's biography, thoroughly examined by many
scholars, lead to such a conclusion.

But eroticism and physical desire are powerful elements of Delius's life
and art, and Aphrodite was surely a sometime companion to those around

him for any length of time. Thomas Ward's poem "Fairy Elves," preserved in one of Delius's notebooks, could suggest experiences at Solano Grove other than endless toil at species counterpoint and listening to plantation songs. The poem mirrors the nineteenth-century American parlor tradition to which it belongs and perhaps also gives us a glimpse of life at Delius's cottage:

Come sprightly fairy elves
Daylight has fled.
Wrap now your tiny selves
In petals red.
Draw from each lily bell
Perfume so fine
Bring from each violet well
Sweet Wine.

Then to the golden crowned
Meadow we'll hie
Circling in merry dance
Sparkling we'll fly.
Under the spreading beach
Then will we throng
Wending a part in each
Sweet Song.

Down from the climbing vine
Lights we will swing
Play while their colors shine
Dance, drink and sing
Tell of the pranks we played
Oft in our grove
On those who came and made
Sweet love.[20]

What should we make of these far from inspired verses? They might suggest sylvan bliss "under the spreading beach" or the visit of nymphets to a lapsing Catholic "in our grove." On the other hand, they might disclose nothing more than Ward's flair for writing sentimental poetry. From what we know about Delius's personality, I suspect the ambience at Solano Grove was at times sexual, and Ward's later decision to join a monastic order—to leave the temptations of a sensual life behind—confirms this suspicion. Secrets of love

and sex must remain, however, on the banks of the St. Johns, where (to quote the better verses of Delius's southern opera *Koanga*) "from magnolia trees the heavy scent is blown, and strange lights wander o'er the dark lagoon."

To continue the story of Ward we must move away from the conjectural hedonistic world of Solano Grove and enter the actual religious world of Jacksonville. What was Ward's daily life like in Jacksonville, and what kinds of music was he involved with?

The Church of the Immaculate Conception, where Ward could be heard at the organ each Sunday, was one of Jacksonville's more handsome buildings, its plain Romanesque structure having been completed and dedicated on March 8, 1873.[21] Shortly after Ward's arrival the white brick church was fitted with a hundred handsome new pews, "finished up in native woods with solid walnut trimmings" and described in the *Times-Union* on July 17, 1884, as "perhaps the handsomest in the State." Ward would soon find a friend in Father William J. Kenny, a fellow New York native three years his senior (b. in 1853 in Delhi, New York) and a priest of deep spiritual convictions. (Kenny came to Jacksonville from the Palatka Mission in August 1884 and remained there until becoming Bishop of the Diocese of St. Augustine in 1902.)

How good was the music of the Church of the Immaculate Conception? What was Ward's reputation in the church? The Jacksonville press indirectly provides answers to these questions. For his first Christmas midnight service, in 1884, the choir presented a mass by a long-forgotten composer, Harrison Millard (1829–1895). The soloists, Mamie Hughes and Susan Weldon-Lund, sopranos, L. C. Emery, tenor, and F. W. Ely, bass, "under the animated touch of the organist, Mr. Ward, filled out a perfect diapason of praise," noted the *Florida Times-Union* on Christmas Day, citing Ward's name in its pages for the first time. At Easter and Christmas the unvarying offerings of mostly insubstantial music (anonymous *veni creators*, *bone pastors*, *adeste fideleses*, etc.) were usually enthusiastically reviewed by the press, which civic-mindedly heaped praise on the city's local talent. At Easter in 1885, for instance, the Immaculate Conception's choir "covered itself with new glory" according to the *Times-Union* of April 7, 1885, and after the Christmas midnight mass that year, heard by "throngs of people," the paper's reviewer gushed about a Mass in B-flat by the prolific Catholic composer Henry Farmer (1819–1891): "It is not saying to[o] much when we declare that there never has been such a

Church of the Immaculate Conception, Jacksonville. (Photo by Daryl Joseph, original in Florida Collection, Jacksonville Public Library.)

grand outburst of musical expression as was heard last night." After midnight mass one year later (1886), the reviewer, unable to invent loftier praise, repeated the same sentence in wonderment at the same mass, directed by Frank Ely, the bass soloist of 1884, and featuring as its principal soloist "Mrs. Walker of New Orleans," who offered the congregation a "bone pastor." These occasional reports, however, can offer only a glimmer of Ward's responsibilities in the services. Any church documents or municipal records that might have provided more information perished in the great Jacksonville fire of May 3, 1901, which completely destroyed the church.[22]

Looking at these old reviews, I can imagine discontent growing in an organist who had recently conducted Haydn and Mozart masses in Brooklyn. The public soon seemed to take Ward, an accompanying organist, for granted at these services. All we know about his role at the midnight mass of 1885 (with the awe-inspiring Farmer music) is the anonymous reviewer's casual observation (after laudatory accounts of the soloists) that "Professor Ward, of course, presided at the organ."[23] Perhaps because of the uninspiring artistic environment, Ward gradually began to move beyond the Catholic Church toward concert and social music, and he befriended several strong personalities who played commanding roles in Jacksonville's cultural life in the 1880s. A look at some of these people provides a clearer picture of Ward's own musical life in Jacksonville.

The most popular soloists at the Catholic Church were the sopranos Florence Keep and her young protégée Rosina Patterson, both deemed to be

"*artistes* in the highest sense of the word."[24] Patterson, like her teacher, specialized in florid coloratura arias, preferably Italian, and possessed a "powerful, but sweet soprano voice," according to the *Times-Union* of April 27, 1887. The paper had heaped even greater praise on her on February 28, 1887, envisioning "the future of a grand artist . . . before her." When performing in concerts with Ward, she invariably stole the show and won the hearts of her audience.

At a benefit concert at the Jacksonville Library Hall on October 17, 1887 (two years after Delius's departure), "Professor Ward" and his pupil, "little Miss Nellie Cummings," began with a piano duet, the overture from Ferdinand Hérold's *Zampa*, "charmingly executed by little Miss Nellie . . . and her proficient instructor," according to the next morning's *Times-Union*. Ward later performed Charles Gimbel Jr.'s variations on Stephen Foster's "Old Black Joe," *Grand Paraphrase de Concert on the Popular Melody*, op. 33 (1877), a pianistic showpiece delivered "in [Ward's] usual easy, artistic style," as the paper phrased it, and which, among the instrumental works heard, the audience "probably listened to with the most pleasure." This curious Gottschalkian imitation by an obscure composer is the only American work played by Ward in Jacksonville in which title and composer can be definitely identified, and it suggests once more that it was the unsophisticated emotionalism of American folk and art music (here combined) that Ward effectively communicated to his audience—and his students. (By coincidence, his former student Delius, at the Leipzig Conservatory, was at that very time composing his *Florida Suite*, in which the American folk style is elevated to art with most of its sterotypes left behind.)

But Ward may have been upstaged on this occasion: later Patterson—who, the reviewer noted, had won "undisputed pre-eminence in musical circles"—stepped downstage and sang "'Tis But a Little Faded Flower," a "little ballad . . . so exquisitely rendered as to receive a double encore and necessitate the denial of a third appearance." Ward could hardly have competed with Patterson with her "sweet arch way and velvety voice."

Another of the Catholic Church soloists frequently mentioned in the press was the basso, Carl von Weller, likewise a specialist in Italian arias from *Il Trovatore* and the like. Von Weller's emotional rendition of the popular song "Some Day" led a reviewer to remark in the *Times-Union* of April 16, 1886, that some of the "auditors" felt they "had been there"—whatever that puzzling comment means. What "some day" eventually held in store for von

Charles Gimbel Jr., "Foster's Old Black Joe: Paraphrase de Concert," op. 33. (Library of Congress.)

Weller, however, was not fame and local acceptance but ruin and disgrace. He fraudulently claimed to be descended from German royalty, to speak several languages fluently, and to have attended the best music conservatories. Although secretly married to a woman in Missouri, he proposed to and attempted the seduction of several young ladies of Jacksonville society. After being arrested for theft, he was brought to trial in Jacksonville and imprisoned for a short while, before eventually coming to a sad end as a suicide in 1889 in Columbia, Pennsylvania.[25]

Announcing a benefit concert to be held on April 15, 1886, the Times-Union suggested on that morning that "with Professor Ward at the piano" and Professor Carl von Weller directing "the stage business," the entire affair would be "in the hands of gentlemen who would make any entertainment a success." The concert was to be staged for the benefit of Jacksonville's most famous musician and Ward's shrewdest rival: Signor Francisco Miglionico, violinist and self-promoter extraordinaire, who "while a 'boy musician'. . . was twice presented with gold medals by Dom Pedro, Emperor of Brazil."

The Italian violinist Miglionico, more than any other musician, best exemplified Jacksonville's attitude toward classical music. Jacksonville, like other provincial southern towns, and like the larger northern cities for that matter, regarded "high musical culture" and "imported from Europe" as synonymous. A good European pedigree, or at least the appearance of one, could gain an individual admittance into the upper levels of society. And Miglionico was the real thing, not to be compared with ersatz Italian prima donnas like Florence Keep[26] and Rosina Patterson or with a masquerading European like von Weller.

Professor Miglionico had settled in Jacksonville in the mid-1880s with his harpist brother and a pianist companion, "Signora L. Armellini." Both Miglionico and Armellini were soon noted approvingly in the press as "musicians of note of the Italian School and natives of the sunny land of song."[27] In the melodramatic words of the *Times-Union*, this "son of Italy" "two or three years ago . . . quietly appeared among us in the most unostentatious manner, unannounced and unheralded, but he brought his violin with him, and he needed no other card of introduction. The smooth and conscientious playing that never drew from the strings a false, careless or unfinished note, could not long remain unrecognized in our music-loving community" (April 16, 1886).

The paper further added that the benefit recital in April was meant to raise funds so that Miglionico and his brother might return to Italy to see their father, who had been "stricken in their transatlantic home." Well publicized, this concert was "intended to excel any ever given in Florida, and perhaps equal any one given in the South."[28] We can imagine the excited expectations of Jacksonville's cultural elite.

Miglionico often played for services at the Immaculate Conception, sometimes to Ward's accompaniment. The two musicians doubtless knew each other well, each taking the full measure of the other's talents. At the April fund-raising concert, those in attendance could have heard Miglionico and Ward perform a violin showpiece, the "Fantaisie Suédoise," op. 23, by Hubert Léonard (1819–1890), and then, as an encore, "Yankee Doodle with some remarkable variations," as the *Times-Union* review of April 16 phrased it. Surely the two virtuosi—the Yankee from Brooklyn and the Italian who had captivated the city—would have been in top form for such an occasion.

Opening the concert, Ward performed Mendelssohn's *Rondo Capriccioso* and "showed himself a faithful interpreter of the music of the great master. . . .

The Professor was encored and obligingly responded," the paper added, not bothering to name the piece. When in the second half of the program Ward began with Chopin's *Fantaisie-Impromptu*, about which the reviewer said nothing, he may have been already overshadowed by Miglionico, who had held the capacity audience "spell bound and breathless." Ward's performance of Mendelssohn and Chopin, the only substantial music on the program, were probably already out of mind when Patterson and "Mr. Farrington" concluded the evening with a duet, "Good Night, My Love." The audience was ecstatic: "All present rose from their seats with a *bon voyage* for the musical brothers in their hearts and a sincere hope that their stay in foreign lands may be short, and the Italy of America claim them again by the opening of another season."

As a pianist, Ward also faced competition from Miglionico's consort, Signora Armellini, known in Jacksonville for her flashy performances. At the October 17, 1886, concert on which Ward played the "Old Black Joe" variations in his relaxed style, Armellini rendered "the grand instrumental composition, Listz's [sic] 'Rhapsodie Hongraise' [sic] . . . in a manner which would have pleased the Master himself could he have heard her faultless execution," according to the astonished *Times-Union* reviewer. Her frequent performances of a Chopin polonaise ("one of the most difficult compositions known to pianists," in the newspaper's estimate) showed "an artiste's conception of the master's work and hands that are skilled in execution, never growing weary of practice."[29] Fifty years later, one Jacksonville resident, Frederikke Mordt-Mencke—who could recollect little of Ward beyond having met him, an "Englishman of tuberculous tendency, and an accomplished music teacher," as she half accurately described him[30]—recalled Armellini vividly: "a brilliant musician . . . a Frenchwoman of noble birth," an honor graduate of the Paris Conservatory who married "a no-good Italian" while studying in Italy.[31]

Among such virtuosi, Ward's "easy, artistic style" and his preference for Americanisms like "Yankee Doodle" and Stephen Foster tunes may have placed him outside the Jacksonville elect. He still occasionally performed with Miglionico, who on Christmas Day of 1886 gave "some exquisite violin renditions" for which "Professor Ward presided at the organ," the *Times-Union* noted. We cannot connect him to the patronage of Delius's German-born friend William Jahn, the dedicatee of his "Zum Carnival," or to A. B. Campbell, the new proprietor of Merryday & Paine's and the publisher of that early Delius piece. In any case, Ward soon began to look to another way to earn his living.

As early as 1875, Jacksonville's larger hotels such as the Everett and the St. James had begun presenting Sunday evening "sacred concerts," programs whose religious repertory was soon replaced by overtures, marches, popular songs of the day, opera potpourris, and other light fare.[32] About the time of Delius's departure, Ward began playing with these society bands. A typical one was Professor Nesbitt's band, which gave weekly concerts in St. James Park, including one on June 11, 1886, promising "sweet music" and including a "Song-Trombone Solo" composed by "Mr. T. Ward," the *Times-Union* noted. Ward's name also appears among the personnel of Professor Rich's orchestra, whose two-hour concert at the YMCA on April 7, 1887, was "assisted by Professor T. F. Ward" at the piano.[33] These "bands" were probably an equivalent of the modern cocktail-hour ensemble and, like their counterparts today, the musicians could find themselves in awkward situations. When, for instance, Professor Nesbitt's band played for the Duval High School commencement exercises in 1886, "Professor Ward at the piano, Mr. Gorham beside the bass viol and Mr. Nesbitt at the clarionette" dutifully punctuated the exercises with music. The musicians and even the guest speaker, Governor Edward A. Perry, waited patiently as Annie Denton read the salutatory on "The Almighty Dollar" and Rosa Sherwood, a sweet-faced young lady from Suwanee, recited the class history—followed appropriately by "Suwanee River" and "Then You'll Remember Me" by the three-piece band, which, like the reporter for the *Times-Union* of June 4, 1886, could give thanks that the summer vacation was at hand. Frivolous as it might seem, Ward's Jacksonville experience as an orchestra player would be important for him later in his life.

Ward was a strong-willed, assertive person in Brooklyn and in the South; at St. John's Home and at Solano Grove he had been accustomed to giving orders and establishing the rules. The moralistic, authoritarian training of St. John's Home occasionally surfaced, even in Jacksonville. The *Times-Union* of February 10, 1886, notes his presence at "Speeches and Songs Galore" given two days earlier by the Magnolia Division of the Sons of Temperance. Though not mentioned as a performer, Ward delivered a speech—a "recitation"—at "one of the most pleasant concerts ever given in connection with temperance work in Jacksonville" by an organization that was "doing good work in lifting many besotted men from the mire and clay of debauched manhood" and establishing them again as "freemen from the bondage of the wine cup."

With Jacksonville's music dominated by foreigners and with a church job offering little challenge, it was perhaps time for an ambitious person to move on. There was no kindred spirit like Delius with whom Ward could communicate, no person with whom to enjoy the simpler music of blacks and Florida "crackers." And those preening, blue-blooded Italians, those "artistes"—might they not have grated on his nerves as time went on?

Circumstantial evidence does, in fact, suggest a personality conflict of some sort at the Church of the Immaculate Conception. On March 14, 1887, the Times-Union printed the following letter to the editor from an anonymous "A. B." involving its star soloist, Rosina Patterson: "Many visitors at the Catholic Church were disappointed today in the absence of Miss Rosina Patterson during high mass. . . . We trust the rumor of some lack of courtesy to Miss Patterson may be without foundation, and that she will resume the place which now seems so truly hers after the ten years she has lent her voice and soul in the praises of her loved church." Might the "lack of courtesy" refer to a clash between Patterson and a bored organist? Not even Father Kenny's acquisition of a "mammoth new organ . . . said to be the largest and most expensive in the State" and first heard "under the masterly hand of Prof. Ward"[34] on February 27 (two weeks before the incident with Patterson was noted) could induce the organist to remain any longer at the church. By Easter 1887, Patterson was back in the fold and Frank Ely was again in charge of the "well trained choir" of the Immaculate Conception, according to the Times-Union of April 11. But Ward was conspicuously absent.

If indeed they existed, the tensions caused by conflicting personalities and unattainable artistic goals would be unhealthy for a consumptive. Moreover, it is likely that in Jacksonville Ward's physical condition began to decline, leading him to move further into Florida. Perhaps also he wanted to escape the new crowds in Jacksonville and the possibility of being caught up in the yellow fever epidemic sweeping through Florida's larger towns in the 1880s (and which would bring devastation to Jacksonville by 1888).

The old town of St. Augustine, forty miles to the south, prided itself on being "free from all malarial influences. No question of bad health can be urged," the Times-Union stated, perhaps enviously, on April 8, 1887.[35] One twenty-year resident, J. D. Lopez, said at the time, "for those who would have long life, good living, good society, it were not easy to find a better spot than the first city settled on this continent, the ancient . . . city of St. Augus-

tine."[36] In 1888, with Jacksonville "one yellow fever hospital," Bishop John Moore observed that St. Augustine had "no sickness whatever. . . . I never knew it to be so healthy."[37] Rev. Moore (1834–1901), Bishop of the Diocese of St. Augustine since 1876 and a staunch supporter of education and the arts, was probably the man responsible for bringing Ward to St. Augustine. With better prospects and a healthier climate before him, in early 1887 Ward found himself in the "Ancient City," as St. Augustine was popularly known, where he assumed the coveted post of organist at the venerable cathedral of the country's oldest diocese. A bright future seemed very probable.

→ As in generations past, St. Augustine, Florida, can today captivate anyone who unexpectedly chances upon it, as I did a few years ago. For those who can forgive its tourist trappings, it remains a town of romance, mystery, and sensuous beauty. More than a century ago, Thomas F. Ward perhaps read in the *Brooklyn Daily Times* about the "time-eaten" Spanish fort and other curiosities of a "City that was Old when the Republic was Born":

> In late years the "Ancient City" or "Augustine" as Floridians style it, has taken on more life and spirit. . . .
>
> In the evening, the city is lighted by kerosene lamps placed in lamp posts. Through the hot sleepy days, donkeys drive their mail carts. . . . High coquina walls enclose the quaint courts, and conceal gardens rich and blooming with Japan plum, grape fruit, fig, date palms, bananas, lemon, and orange and every variety of fruit and flower congenial to tropical climate and soil. From these old Spanish homes, while passing through the quaint, narrow streets, you hear occasionally issue the sweet sound of the guitar, the harp or the piano, mingling with melodious soprano or tenor voices, and it suggests to the mind the fandangoes, bal masques, troubadours, serenades . . . of sunny and passionate Spain, and a feeling seizes you that you would like to live in St. Augustine all your life. You realize these and other romantic suggestions day and night. Perhaps a long residence in the ancient town would dispel these illusions, perhaps not. (January 6, 1883)

A. J. R., the Brooklyn correspondent, added that St. Augustine was "the least built up city I have yet seen in Florida." In 1887, the year Ward moved there, it was a town of about 3,200 year-round inhabitants, according to the *Florida State Gazetteer and Business Directory for 1886–87*. Founded by the Spaniards in 1565,

St. Augustine, view of the city, 1885. (St. Augustine Historical Society.)

and with more than three centuries of conflict between Spanish, British, and Americans in its past, the city had attracted better-educated consumptives since Florida's entry into the Union in 1845.

One of those with weak lungs, the poet Sidney Lanier had traveled through St. Augustine a decade before Ward; in 1876 Lanier observed that the distance from Jacksonville to St. Augustine was "the distance from the nineteenth century to the sixteenth" and that the difference between the two cities was the difference between the "vim of Andrew Jackson" and the "saintly contemplation" of Pedro Menéndez de Avilés, founder of the Spanish colony. Lanier described its languorous atmosphere to perfection:

A sailor has just yawned.

It is seven o-clock, of an April morning such as does not come anywhere in the world except at St. Augustine or on the Gulf Coast of Florida . . . a morning which mingles infinite repose with infinite glittering, as if God should smile in his sleep. . . .

For here the east wind, of such maleficent reputation in the rest of the world, redeems all its brethren. . . . One finds no difficulty in believing that in the course of a few years the entire population of the earth and of the heavens above the earth and the waters beneath the earth would be settled in and around this quaint, romantic, straggling, dear and dearer-growing city of St. Augustine.

Intersection of Treasury and Charlotte Streets, St. Augustine, 1886. (St. Augustine Historical Society.)

Pre-Flagler St. Augustine, with the old Spanish fort and city gates. (Archives of St. Joseph's Convent, St. Augustine.)

As for St. Augustine's advantages for good health, Lanier enthusiastically recommended the city to his fellow sufferers: "Most consumptives, particularly those who have passed the earlier stage of the disease, are said to find the air of St. Augustine too 'strong' in midwinter, but to enjoy its climate greatly in April and May." But above all he counseled: "Be brave with your consumption: do not discuss it with bated breath. . . . Endeavor to have some occupation consistent with your disease's requirement. Brooding kills." Lanier even recommended getting out into the wilderness. "Kill alligators and sell their teeth" if it helps you, he urged.[38]

St. Augustine could cast the same spell on a robber baron from the North as on a Georgia poet or a Jacksonville organist, and Ward's arrival would follow by only one year that of the arch-capitalist and cofounder of the Standard Oil Company, Henry Morrison Flagler (1830–1913). Flagler, who had fallen in love with the city on his first visit in 1877, saw in Florida in the late 1880s an unprecedented opportunity for the investment of capital. His luxury hotels and pioneering railroads would soon transform Florida from America's most primitive wilderness into a modern state. When Ward moved to the city in 1887, the resplendent Ponce de Leon Hotel, begun in 1885, was nearing completion and the Alcazar, of almost equal luxuriousness, was under construction.[39] Because of Flagler the trip from Jacksonville to St. Augustine, formerly an eight-hour journey by riverboat and overland, could now be made by rail and ferry in ninety minutes.[40]

Ward's circumstances had dramatically improved. Not only could he live in a Catholic city, free of the religious prejudice of the South, but he could also enjoy the musical culture of the North in a town where the arts had begun to flourish. Shortly before Easter 1887 he settled in the Ancient City and joined a Catholic tradition that could trace its heritage back to the sixteenth century.

The new organist successfully carried out his musical responsibilities at the cathedral. Though not citing his name, the *St. Augustine Press* mentioned on April 16 that on Easter Sunday "the Cathedral was uncommonly crowded, chairs having been placed in the aisles to accommodate the unusual attendance," and it singled out the music as "superb" and reflecting "unbounded credit on the choir."

Upon arrival in St. Augustine, Ward immediately placed an advertisement in the *St. Johns County Weekly*, a local newspaper:

Learn to Sing at Sight

Thos. F. Ward, Organist at the Cathedral, has organized a singing class which will meet once a week. Those desirous of thorough instruction should join at once. A few pupils will also be received for private instruction in sight reading, or on the piano or organ. For particulars address T. F. Ward, care of F. Sultzner [sic], City. April 9, 1887. (April 9 and 16, 1887)

Like Merryday & Paine's in Jacksonville, Frederick Sulzner's piano shop quickly became Ward's center of operations. Located on the south side of Treasury Street (between Spanish and St. George Streets), the store was practically next door to the cathedral. A music teacher himself, Frederick Sulzner (1823–1899) sold, in addition to pianos and organs, "clocks, jewelry, sewing machines, machine oil," and other merchandise. Ward's responsibility was to provide the "tuition in vocal and instrumental music" that Sulzner's own advertisements promoted.[41]

Everything seemed to point toward a satisfying new life for Ward. But only two days after that splendid Easter, as his ad was going to press, a catastrophic event, remembered to this day in St. Augustine, brought his new career to a sudden end. In the early hours of Tuesday, April 12, 1887, flames

The Cathedral, St. Augustine, ca. 1886. (Archives of St. Joseph's Convent, St. Augustine.)

"The St. Augustine Hotel, Cathedral, and Old Slave Market before the Fire." (*Harper's Weekly*, April 23, 1887.)

broke out in the laundry room of the St. Augustine Hotel. The fire quickly spread out of control, and by early morning many blocks in the town's center lay in ruins. On April 13, a Jacksonville reporter described the tragedy in the *Florida Times-Union*: "The old, venerable and ancient landmark, the Spanish Cathedral was doomed, and it went down amid the tornado of destruction, the old chimes being powerless after pealing out their warning to get the aid necessary to save its venerated walls, the very clock daring to strike the last half hour while surrounded by flames—at 5:30—which were lifting up its hands for the last time on earth."

Only the cathedral's walls remained standing. Other buildings damaged in the conflagration included Sulzner's music store (with Ward's studio), which sustained a loss of a thousand dollars worth of uninsured goods, according to the same Jacksonville correspondent. (The *St. Augustine Press* reported three days later that the first estimates of fire losses were exaggerated and placed Sulzner's losses at only three hundred dollars.) One minor consequence of this tragedy was that Sulzner temporarily removed his store to Palatka and did not reopen it in St. Augustine until almost four months later, when he installed it in the building of Bertola Genovar's Opera House at 11 St. George Street near the Old City Gate.[42] Ward's church job and his business headquarters had vanished overnight.

The loss of the old cathedral brought a deep and lingering sadness to the city. An anonymous poet lamented in the Jacksonville paper two months afterward:

Tolls now no more the old Cathedral bells,
Where mellow golden notes for ages past
Have rung forth wedding chimes and sad
  death knells.
The sounds have hushed; the shrine is gone
  at last.[43]

If these words reflected the emotion of an average citizen, we can imagine the distress experienced by Thomas Ward, who had everything at stake in St. Augustine. With the cathedral gone, Catholic services were temporarily held at the convent of the Sisters of St. Joseph on St. George Street. Just after the calamity, Ward placed the following notice in the *St. Johns County Weekly* on April 16: "There will be three Masses at the Convent on Sunday; at 6:30, 8:00 and 10:00 local time. Confessions will be heard at the Convent this afternoon at 3 o'clock. T. F. Ward."[44]

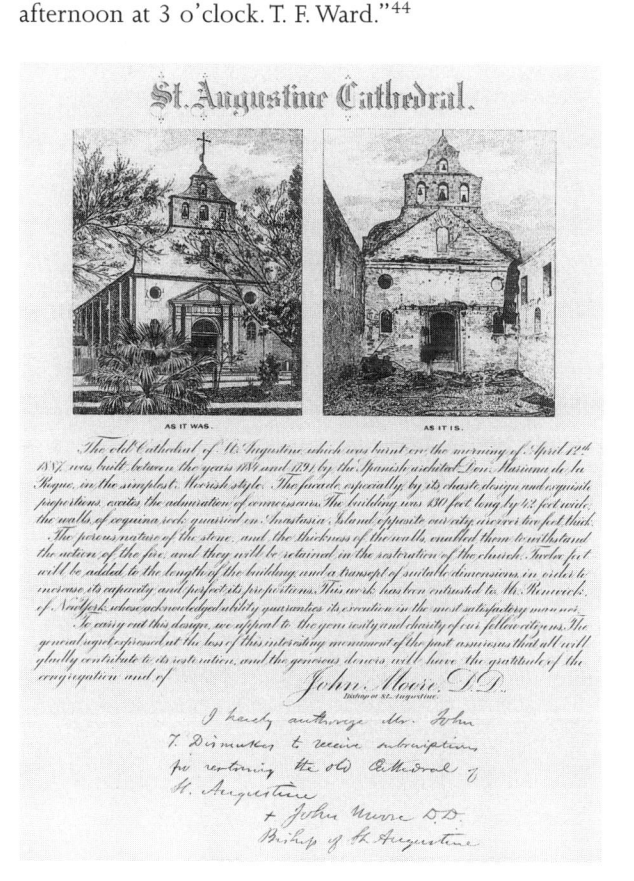

Cathedral of St. Augustine before and after the Great Fire of 1887. (Archives of St. Joseph's Convent, St. Augustine.)

It is ironic that ill fortune brought Ward again into close association with the Sisters of St. Joseph, who, in Brooklyn, had been his guardians in an earlier time of crisis. Having settled in St. Augustine in 1866, the Sisters had occupied their beautiful coquina convent since 1876 and were a vital part of the religious and educational life of the town, where their charity and industry were cherished by the community.

With the fire of 1887, my search for Thomas F. Ward confronted many obstacles. In the period from 1886 to 1888, only eight single editions of St. Augustine newspapers have survived. I now had to rely on condensed weekly regional reports in the Jacksonville newspapers, none of which gives a clue as to how long Ward remained at his post of cathedral organist. But we know that the place of music in the cathedral's services was minimal for almost two years—surely a dispiriting development for Ward. During the Christmas season nine months after the fire, when music should have been highlighted, the Florida Times-Union of December 26, 1887, commented that because of the fire and the limited space of the Convent, "for the first time since the construction of the Old Cathedral . . . the customary celebration of midnight mass has been omitted."

Circumstantial evidence seems to suggest that Thomas Ward either resigned or was released from his organist post at some time in 1887–88 during the difficult period when the cathedral was being rebuilt. On December 22, 1888, almost two years after the fire, the Times-Union announced that St. Augustine's cathedral had "risen from the ashes more magnificent and beautiful than ever" and was in possession of a "great Pilcher Brothers organ . . . costing $7,000." According to the paper, the new organ "would have been erected long ago had it not been tied up in a Jacksonville warehouse awaiting the cessation of the [yellow fever] epidemic to be transported." The instrument was heralded in St. Augustine as "undoubtedly the finest organ in the State."[45] No organist is named. But Ward would surely not have willingly quit the cathedral after it acquired such a superb instrument. Perhaps he had already left by then. There seems to be no solution to the puzzle. Whatever the case, around Thanksgiving of 1889, Lewis Clarke, a local musician active in Flagler's society orchestras, was hired as organist and baritone soloist, according to the St. Augustine Weekly News of November 28, and held Ward's former post for several years.

At this point, the mystery surrounding Thomas F. Ward begins to deepen. From economic necessity, he occasionally showed up in Jacksonville to per-

form in musical events like those described earlier. After October 1887, however, his name disappears altogether from Jacksonville's newspapers. Where
was he? He took no part in the numerous music events of the Florida Sub-
Tropical Exposition of 1888 in Jacksonville, in which the ubiquitous Francisco Miglionico played the principal role. Nor is his name among the
well-trained musicians of Flagler's hotel orchestras, whose performances the
Jacksonville press often covered. Indeed, Flagler himself had little sympathy
for those afflicted with tuberculosis. On a visit to St. Augustine in 1882, he
expressed delight that the old San Marco Hotel was filled "not with consumptives, but [with] that class of society one meets at the great watering
places of Europe—men who go there to enjoy themselves and not for the
benefit of their health."[46] It is unlikely that the entrepreneur Flagler, who
supervised the tiniest details of his hotel operations, would have permitted
Ward to be hired, orchestral experience and superior musical abilities not-
withstanding.

An obscure 1889 statewide directory lists "T. F. Ward" as a "Music Teacher"
dwelling in St. Augustine but gives no specific residence.[47] The absence of a
street address can be explained: when the directory appeared, Ward had been
staying on and off in the Carleton Hotel, located at the corner of St. George
and Treasury Streets, only a stone's throw from the ruined cathedral and vir-
tually in the shadow of the Ponce de Leon Hotel.

The small but elegant Carleton had been opened to the public in October
1887 by Wilson Michael Teahen of Sanford, Florida. The Canadian-born
Teahen, a friend of General Henry S. Sanford, was an industrious real estate
investor who had moved up from Sanford to take over several small St. Augustine hotels. As the Carleton's four surviving ledger books show, Teahen
administered the establishment efficiently and concerned himself with the
comfort of his guests. In addition to rooms (offered "en suite or single")
and board "at liberal terms" (two to three dollars per week), he provided a
nurse for the occupants and at times had a doctor on the premises. The Carleton
was, as his advertisement announced, "strictly first class."[48]

The hotel's ledgers offer a glimpse of Thomas Ward's life after the cathedral fire. From July 18 to August 17, 1888, "Prof. Ward," a "regular boarder,"
paid five dollars weekly for room and board, both in cash and "tuition" (i.e.,
music lessons), and on departing, closed out his account of $20.16 for those
four weeks.[49] Again, from January 21 through February 16, 1889, Ward took
meals at the hotel, possibly leaving behind temporarily an unpaid bill of

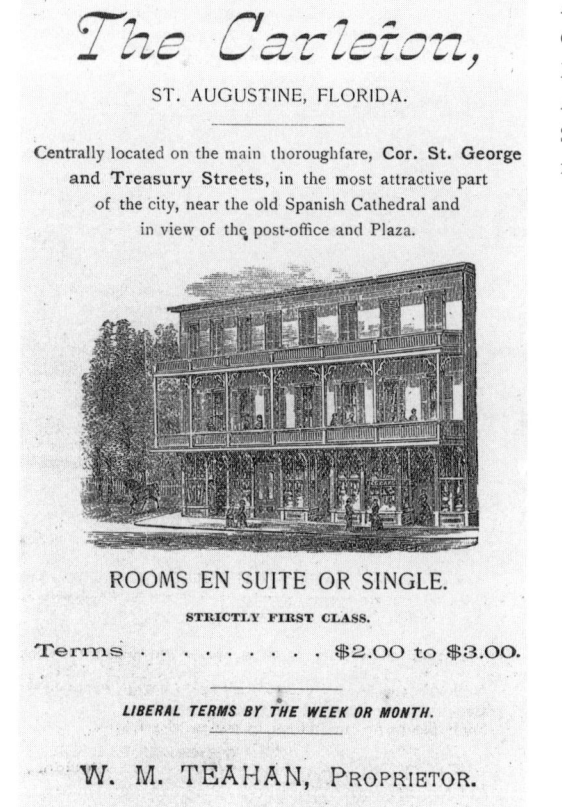

The Carleton,

ST. AUGUSTINE, FLORIDA.

Centrally located on the main thoroughfare, **Cor. St. George and Treasury Streets**, in the most attractive part of the city, near the old Spanish Cathedral and in view of the post-office and Plaza.

ROOMS EN SUITE OR SINGLE.

STRICTLY FIRST CLASS.

Terms . . . . $2.00 to $3.00.

LIBERAL TERMS BY THE WEEK OR MONTH.

W. M. TEAHAN, Proprietor.

Advertisement for the Carleton Hotel from *Popular Health Resorts of the South.* (St. Augustine Historical Society.) Teahen's name is misspelled.

$4.35.[50] Since his account was not credited and marked with the bold "OFF" with which Teahen ended each transaction, it is possible that Ward was having financial problems in early 1889.

More significantly, Teahen's ledgers furnish evidence that Ward was unwell during 1888. His sickness—surely consumption—can be deduced from the proprietor's account for "Nellie the Nurse." According to his "Servants' Time Book," Teahen employed Nellie (her surname is unknown) from December 1887 to June 1888 and then suddenly called her back to service after six weeks, on July 16, 1888, just as Ward registered at the hotel. The faithful Nellie was paid six dollars per week for her services and then released again one month later—at the exact time Ward paid his bill and left.[51] (In 1889 Dr. Dewitt Webb, a prominent local physician, boarded at the Carleton and would have offered medical services to its lodgers, but no definite link between him and Ward can be established.[52])

The Carleton Hotel, St. Augustine, ca. 1886. (Courtesy Mrs. Marjorie Blaskower.)

We can presume that Ward lived in other of Teahen's hotels, such as "Miss Hasseltine's Boarding House," open during the "season" (December through May),[53] or took rooms in the largest of them, the "Florida House," purchased by Teahen in April 1886.[54] Restless and moving frequently, he was struggling to regain his health and find financial security in the rapidly changing town. But he could no longer conceal his tuberculosis, and consequently, his opportunities of finding pupils must have diminished—or vanished. In Jacksonville from 1884 to 1887, Ward had been a highly visible public figure, known to the entire music community, but in St. Augustine, he became an outsider, a recluse, another health-endangering consumptive.

A century later, in 1986, Ward remained an enigma, eluding all my efforts to find him. In August of that year Sister Mary Albert Lussier took me to the chapel in the St. Joseph's Convent where Ward had attended mass almost a century before. In search of his presence in the Ancient City, I kept returning to the town that seemed to symbolize the mystery of Thomas F. Ward—a place (for me) still haunted by his presence there a century before. But my search produced only an unfocused, shaded portrait of a lonely, ill man. John Redmond, owner of the St. George Pharmacy, a drugstore near Sulzner's music

shop even in Ward's day, kindly allowed me to rummage through century-old prescriptions in the hope of finding medicines prescribed for a tubercular musician—to no avail. "How could this gifted man have retreated into complete anonymity?" I kept asking. My searches through cathedral, municipal, court, and hospital records in St. Johns County produced absolutely nothing more about Ward. No one in St. Augustine with ties to the Flagler era remembers anything of him or of ancestors who knew him. In St. Augustine, he is a forgotten man.

Perhaps the very lack of documentation tells us something about the misfortune descending on Thomas F. Ward. For someone suffering from tuberculosis, catastrophic events can bring about a sudden turn for the worse and often, too, mood swings and depression. It is likely that the professional crisis precipitated by the fire of 1887 did just that, forcing him for three years into a financially precarious existence as an unnoticed music teacher.[55]

He now repeated what had become a pattern of behavior: when his tuberculosis was revealed, he either withdrew into himself or moved on. Around 1890, Ward fell back on the business skills learned during his Brooklyn college days and, severing his ties with the Ancient City, moved farther south into Florida's wilderness. In 1891, "Professor Ward" surfaced in Orlando, where he earned his living as a bookkeeper for the *Orlando Daily Record* and occupied rooms in the Arcade Hotel on Robinson Avenue in that small town of 5,000 people.[56] We can assume that he faithfully attended mass at the newly built St. James Church on Orange Avenue nearby.

Life's vicissitudes had brought Thomas F. Ward from the prestige of his musical profession in Brooklyn to the obscurity of a clerical position in remote central Florida. Where could he turn from here? At the edge of the world, perhaps he could simply withdraw from it. Of the two things that had mattered most—his music and his faith—music had brought him precious little. Maybe it was still not too late to find a deeper, meaningful life in the other.

A pioneering group of monks at St. Leo, near the German Catholic community of San Antonio, north of Tampa, had recently settled in Florida and might offer such an opportunity, a way out of the impasse. In 1891 Thomas F. Ward arrived at the priory and college of St. Leo, where as "Frater Paul," a religious cleric, he left the secular world behind and entered into the spiritual life of a Benedictine monastery.

Ward's friendship with Fritz Delius was now six years in the past. Unknown to him, Delius, a graduate of the Leipzig Conservatory, a Parisian citizen of the world, stood in 1891 at the doorway of artistic maturity, the influences of America and Scandinavia soon to blend into a secure musical vision. The musical mastery of *Appalachia* lay only a few years ahead. But what did the future hold for Tom Ward, the thirty-five-year-old would-be monk who had helped Delius arrive at that position and now wanted to find fulfillment in religious devotion? Perhaps the dawn would soon be breaking. But would the radiant morn be nigh? Like the slave singer of *Appalachia*, Thomas F. Ward faced an uncertain future.

↱ *St. Leo Monastery*

"Lives appearing gentle may be hard."
—THOMAS F. WARD

On a sunny Monday in August 1986, I drove onto the grounds of St. Leo Abbey close by the old village of San Antonio, thirty-five miles northeast of Tampa. The blue waters of Lake Jovita were especially inviting on that hot morning. Though nearly a century had passed since Ward had come here, it still seemed that in this part of central Florida, no place "more beneficial to mind and body could be found. Orange and lemon groves everywhere lend a peculiar charm to the natural beauty of the scenery. Deep lakes with clear, cool water abound . . . a never-ceasing source of health and pleasure."[1] As one visitor to the area observed in 1891, the year of Ward's arrival: "San Antonio is built on a succession of plateaux which overlook fair valleys, where lakes nestle like jewels on the bosom of an elfin maid. It is one of the best farming portions and orange growing regions of the State, and whichever way one looks, fair pictures, framed in backgrounds of green pine or azure sky meet the eye."[2] The lovely view had remained remarkably unspoiled in the passing years.

In my excitement at having found his monastery, I searched out the abbey cemetery, certain I would soon find the burial place of Thomas Francis Ward among the monks resting there and finally solve the mystery of his fate. But as in so many previous walks in Florida's cemeteries, my search was futile. "How naïve!" the old monks' tombs seemed to taunt.

The timing of my arrival at St. Leo Abbey, too, seemed inauspicious. Though sympathetic toward my research, Father Henry Riffle, the archivist, had suddenly been called to military service for two years and had recently left the monastery. No one, in fact, was minding the abbey's large archives.

Monastery and College building of St. Leo Priory, ca. 1893, seen from Lake Jovita. (Photo by James J. Horgan, original in St. Leo Archives.)

Without an appointment, I nonetheless found my way to Abbot Patrick Shelton's office and began describing to him the purpose of my unexpected visit. (Surprise, I had reasoned, might be the best strategy in such unfamiliar surroundings.) The abbot seemed puzzled that someone would concern himself with a resident of their community's earliest years. In the midst of his busy morning schedule, and a bit annoyed and distracted—he was purchasing food supplies for the brothers—he instructed his secretary, Brother Joachim, to go and fetch any files on Thomas Francis Ward, alias "Frater Peter," as I had explained. Gentle Brother Joachim soon returned with a single folder marked "Ward" and the monastery's ancient daybook containing the official minutes of the Order of St. Benedict in Florida from its first days. Periodically looked in upon by the abbot, who amusedly admonished me for being preoccupied with insignificant worldly details, I read with astonishment documents that suddenly opened the door to Ward's life, if not completely, at least wider than I had ever imagined possible. Original letters in his hand, probably viewed by no one for almost a century, now told me of an unhappy life at St. Leo and an inability to get along with comrades; the monks' account in their daybook revealed to me their dissatisfaction with a difficult and eccentric personality.

How had Ward found himself in such a strange place, I wondered, and how could an anachronistic Catholic monastery ever have come to exist in an isolated part of Protestant Florida? Attempting to find answers, I soon discovered that St. Leo Abbey was an eminent religious establishment that had strongly influenced the region's life and culture.

Catholicism is deeply rooted in west central Florida. When Ward arrived there, the area was already (after Jacksonville and St. Augustine) the most populous Catholic community in the Florida peninsula. An unlikely chain of circumstances created this anomalous situation. With the blessing of Pope Pius IX, the State of Florida in 1882 granted Edmund F. Dunne (a former Chief Justice of Arizona) 100,000 acres in present-day Pasco County to establish the "Catholic Colony of San Antonio." About half of Judge Dunne's original colonists were German Catholic immigrants, whose cultural influence is still strongly felt.

To this energetic population was soon to be added a second tradition going back to sixth-century Italy, when St. Benedict (480–543) gathered his followers and established the famous Benedictine monastery at Monte Cassino. The Benedictine Rule—to give honor and praise to God in an eremetic life of prayer and work as a counterbalance to evil in the world—has been the basis of Western monasticism from then to the present. To attain spiritual fulfillment a monk must follow St. Benedict's admonition to become a stranger to the ways of this world (*a sacueli actibus se facere alienum*). In the words of the Cistercian monk Thomas Merton, he must achieve "Simple Intention": the desire to seek "the supreme poverty of having nothing but God."[3] Primitive conditions like those in frontier Florida could help a cloistered community achieve this difficult goal.

The Benedictines appeared in central Florida in 1884 when, at the invitation of Bishop John Moore, monks from St. Vincent Archabbey in Latrobe, Pennsylvania, took control of the local Catholic mission. In 1888, they in turn transferred jurisdiction to Maryhelp Abbey in Belmont, North Carolina. By 1890 two priests, one cleric, and four lay brothers were settled into the new monastery, and "St. Leo's college [was] in course of erection."[4]

St. Leo Monastery and its school were officially founded on June 4, 1889, when the Florida legislature granted the Order of St. Benedict a charter to "have and possess the right and power of conferring the usual academic and other degrees granted by any college in this State."[5] On land donated by Judge Dunne, St. Leo Military College opened its doors on September 14, 1890, with four faculty members (Benedictine priests) and thirty-two students who payed two hundred dollars yearly for board and tuition.[6] The school had been named for St. Leo the Great, Pope Leo XIII, and Rev. Leo Haid of Maryhelp Abbey, its first president. Its prospectus described the newly completed buildings as "spacious, well lighted, and ventilated and supplied

with every requisite for a comfortable students' home";[7] the three-story college and monastery building, with its hundred-foot tower and cupola, could be seen from miles away. The school was not completely isolated, for, since 1888, the Orange Belt Railroad passed along the shore of nearby Lake Jovita on its route to St. Petersburg.

Thomas Ward might have known about the new Catholic colony a decade earlier when Dunne's exotically flavored articles, "Prospecting Florida," appeared in the Brooklyn *Catholic Review*, alongside reports mentioning Ward's youthful activities. He probably knew of the college firsthand from Bishop Moore, who, in a letter of endorsement of July 19, 1890, gave it his "hearty approbation . . . as it will bring to our doors opportunities for a higher education for our Catholic young men and boys." Ward was well qualified to teach the school's business curriculum, as well as music, and surely seized the opportunity to be a part of Florida's first Catholic college, especially one administered by music-loving Benedictines.

Ward may also have believed the area would be beneficial to his deteriorating health. The Jacksonville newspaper opined that in these Florida highlands "a more healthy region cannot, in all probability, be found on earth"; the college grounds and the surrounding hills and valleys "recall to the traveller some of the most favored spots of romantic Europe."[8] The Archabbot in Latrobe regarded his new priory as "a Sanitarium for invalid Members of the American Cassinese Congregation of the Benedictine Order." However, some members, drawn to St. Leo from distant abbeys, would not be lucky, and five monks would die of tuberculosis between 1889 and 1898. Ward was more fortunate. In contrast to the humid flatness of the Orlando area, the hilly surroundings of St. Leo were ideal for his health, and an improved physical condition is evidenced by the fact that, three years after his arrival, he helped construct the "cap tower" that replaced the main building's original cupola.[9]

His prior sojourn in Orlando would have remained unknown had an obscure newspaper notice in the St. Leo Archives not come to light: "Prof. Thomas F. Ward, formerly bookkeeper for the *Daily Record*, Orlando is going to St. Leo College at St. Leo, Fla. where he will teach a class in music" during the academic year beginning September 1891.[10]

Assuming the monastic name "Frater Paul," Ward, in 1891–92, instructed the school's forty-two students in "Third commercial, Music and Shorthand" courses. "Paul Ward of New York" was himself a student in "First Philosophy" (i.e., theology), one of two "scholastics"[11] (persons preparing for the

priesthood) who were addressed as "Frater"—as opposed to the lay "brothers." (His fellow scholastic was the nineteen-year-old, Bavarian-born George Schwarz, Frater Dominic, who was to die of tuberculosis in 1898 at age twenty-five, only months after becoming a priest.)

Frater Paul's first responsibility was to guide the students—some as young as eight or nine—through a three-year curriculum of commercial and liberal arts courses culminating in the degree "Master of Accounts." Whatever Ward's influence may have been, the quality of St. Leo's instruction progressed steadily, and on April 15, 1894, the *Times-Union*, Florida's leading newspaper, assessed that St. Leo's "commercial department is equal to that of any institution in the state, to say the least, and its classical, musical and scientific departments are all that can possibly be expected." St. Leo's quasi-military regimen probably reminded Ward of St. John's Home and the orphan cadets of Brooklyn. Military drill was obligatory and diligently conducted by "the Sons of St. Benedict," who, according to the abbot, "had ever been foremost in the ranks of Educators and Christianizers of the world," as the nearby *San Antonio Herald* reported on January 11, 1893. The students wore uniforms combining both gray and blue colors, a lingering reminder of the Civil War, with which the vanquished South had not yet come to terms.

Two men crucial to St. Leo's growth had arrived in 1890, one year before Ward: Rev. Charles H. Mohr, O.S.B. (1863–1931), rector of the college and (after 1894) prior of the monastery, and Father Benedict Roth, O.S.B. (1862–1925), scholar, archivist, and chronicler. The two monks were to become "the pillars on which Saint Leo rested . . . the two St. Leo Gibraltars"[12] and would exert a deep influence on Ward's life there.

Twenty-eight years old when he reached St. Leo Monastery, Father Benedict had taken his vows at Maryhelp Abbey in 1886 and established a reputation as a dedicated teacher and meticulous scholar; he later became a noted historian of the Catholic Church in Florida. Austere and introverted by nature, he kept a private journal and chronology of daily life at St. Leo from 1890 to 1906, the monastery's most valuable record of its pioneer days. The dour Roth took an instant dislike to his fellow-scholar Ward, and on September 26, 1891, noted sarcastically in his journal that Frater Paul and two other monks had "all three got the scholastic habit on arriving." As Ward established a rapport with the students, relations between the reclusive Roth and the more outgoing Ward became more strained; Father Benedict's remarks (confided to his diary) grew more abrasive as years passed.

Father Charles Mohr was cut from a different fabric. He was born in Ohio in 1863 and ordained into the priesthood at Maryhelp Abbey in 1888. As Prior of St. Leo Monastery (and after 1902, its first abbot), Father Charles was the single most powerful personality in molding the institution, which under his guidance was recognized by the Vatican as an independent priory in 1894 and eventually elevated to an abbey in 1902. Seven years Ward's junior, he was a courageous and decisive man, handsome and charismatic, and numbered many famous people among his acquaintances—including Theodore Roosevelt, whom he befriended in 1905. In an old monastery photograph, the man who sits astride his favorite horse, "Tom," gazing out sternly with riding whip in hand, was not—we can plainly see—a person who would put up with rebellious behavior or have his authority challenged.[13] Father Charles insisted on the rigorous military milieu of the school, but he was also fair-minded and showed sympathy for artistic and scholarly endeavors. He played bass fiddle, "tenor" (baritone) horn, organ, and piano, having taught the latter when on the faculty of St. Mary's College at Maryhelp Abbey. For Thomas Ward, Father Charles embodied contradictory symbols: he was a younger father figure for an older Ward, a masculine symbol of authority absent from Ward's youth among the Sisters of St. Joseph, a person to be obeyed but challenged, a proponent of the communal family in a family-less institution. But Mohr inspired love and fealty, too, among his brother monks and students. As Father Benedict observed on New Year's Eve 1894: "Regarding college life at St. Leo's, it must be said to the great credit of Rt. Rev. Fr. Charles that he always treated the students—and inculcated the same— as children of the monastic family . . . and this feature endeared the boys to him very deservedly. Hence it will readily be seen why there was always such a good spirit at St. Leo's."

One wonders what the newly arrived Ward thought of the primitive monastery. He must have been shocked on finding conditions so drastically opposed to the daily comforts and sparkling conversations of Jacksonville, Solano Grove, and St. Augustine. If he sought discipline in thought and work, however, he had come to the right place. The monks were up at 3:45 to begin a long day of religious devotion and hard labor. Many decades later, Father Jerome Wisniewski (1885–1966), reminisced about the founders of St. Leo College: "The faculty wore shoes, but not all of them wore socks. There wasn't enough in the till for that comfort. However, there was enough to eat and drink (homemade scuppernong wine) for the faculty. They raised enough

cabbage, carrots, lettuce, cucumbers and sweet potatoes for the table. Meat was abundant because it cost only three cents a pound on the hoof. . . . Quail coveys were numerous in the piney neighborhood of the college, and hunting dogs and guns at service."[14] Father Jerome added that "the faculty of this pioneer school were not on a reducing diet, but chronically on a reduced bank budget."

Accustoming himself to the harsh circumstances, Ward soon became an outstanding teacher at the military college and endeared himself to his students, who themselves had to be up and about by 5:30. To provide them with moral guidance, he made a list of "Class Mementoes of the Cardinal Virtues," with the intent of associating prudence, justice, temperance, and fortitude with their everyday activities. Frater Paul stressed that one's daily schoolwork could be affixed to the greatest spiritual values—as follows:

> Algebra.—Let s equal success in business, and b your conduct in life; then b2
> = s. This is for Prudence.
> Stenography.—When you may help yourself without injuring another, use
> Longhand; when you can't, use Shorthand. This is for Justice.
> Geometry.—Always remember that a straight line is the shortest distance
> between two points. This is for Fortitude.

Last—and not in the same sequence as the cardinal virtues themselves—he imparted to the youngsters the most important message of all:

> Arithmetic.—What is the ratio between countless gains at the highest per
> cent, and the loss of your immortal soul? This is for Temperance.[15]

Did Ward really equate lack of temperance with the loss of one's immortal soul? Perhaps this was a coded message that concealed a personal secret: he owed his own existence to another's absence of temperance.

Ward held firm if idiosyncratic views about the educational process. He regarded exams as "tests of character" in which "the generosity, manliness and fortitude of the students are tried in a peculiar fashion." In the spring of 1892 for the San Antonio village newspaper, he carefully set down his thoughts about teaching:

> There is such infinite variety of ways in which questions may be pro-
> pounded, that a professor can either stir up a decided spirit of resistance
> in a class, or conduct his examination with great pleasure to the students.

In the former case, the questions will be either so general that even the author of the text-book would find it impossible to condense an appropriate answer; or so muddy that it would need a hundred filters to make the main point of a subject transparent. On the other hand, the question may be so pointed that no one can fail to see its tendency and so limited in its scope that often a monosyllable will suffice for the answer. And here is where a teacher can impress it upon the minds of his pupils that he has it in his power to make them feel their want of application.[16]

The remark about a "want of application" brings to mind his former student Delius. Perhaps the atmosphere of Solano Grove can also be detected in Ward's opinion of St. Leo's quarterly school examinations, expressed in the same article: "[Examinations] are to the school year what the various wines and liquors are to a French dinner—they give a zest to what follows as well as a relish for what has just been received." This refined attitude seems worlds removed from the sentiments of pioneer monks. It is the character of the former Thomas F. Ward, not "Frater Paul," that is revealed.

Emphasizing strict discipline, Frater Paul sometimes gently scolded his students, some of whom were Cubans sent to Florida to learn English in preparation for commercial careers. The *Florida Times-Union* observed on April 15, 1894, that soon after St. Leo's was established "the fame of the college reached the Pearl of the Antilles." A typical humorous newspaper report about the Cubans' language problem appeared in the *San Antonio Herald* on January 18, 1893: "Item: Ramon Rivero, the latest recruit, of Ybor City [now in Tampa], is catching on to English. 'You see,' says he, 'I is Americ.'"[17]

While recognizing each student's educational shortcomings and individual temperament, Ward did not overlook his talents and potentialities. For fellow-seminarian George Schwarz (who was also his student), he composed affectionate limericks about the ten students of his beginning class in commerce, inscribing the new "Class Mementoes."

Dear George,

Whenever you read these lines and recall the Classmates and Professors of your College days of 1892–1893, raise your mind and heart to God in prayer, that we may all attain the end for which we were created.

Affectionately,

Fr. Paul[18]

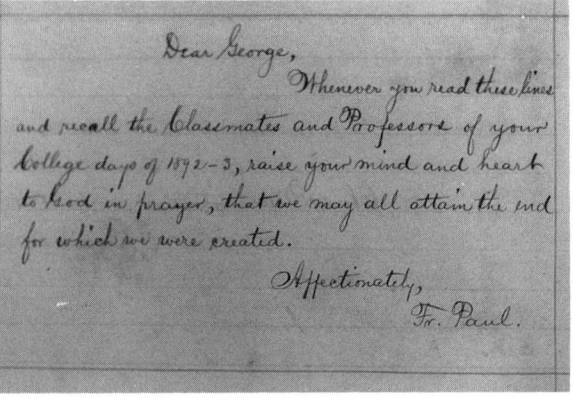

Dedication of Thomas F. Ward's "Class Mementoes of the Cardinal Virtues," 1893. (Photo by James J. Horgan, original in St. Leo Archives.)

In his "Mementoes" Ward laughed with—not at—his pupils; in them he tells us about both himself and his students. A grim but well-intentioned George Davis of Jacksonville lacked the most essential Ward requirement: will power.

Hail, frowning Geordie, whom we'll dub "I can't"
    With brain quite capable, though sluggish will.
How many a story-book thine eyes have scanned
    In classroom, 'twould take several lines to fill.
Yet over-willing hast thou e'er been found,
    When kindness called thee on some other ground.

A fun-loving Charley Sanchez of St. Augustine got a similar chiding for his lack of resolve to learn:

Well, Charley, meekest, gentlest of the crowd,
    Thy tricks were played for sympathy with all;
For where the play was funniest, when most loud,
    We ever found thee prompt at mischief's call.
Thy will to learn might shame the brightest here
    Which ceased when vain the effort did appear.

Neither did Oscar Kennerly, the salutatorian of the first graduating class (1893), measure up to Ward's standards: "Yet must thou own, good Oscar, thou didst fail / Of best endeavors learning's height to scale." Harry Genovar's spunky behavior elicited the sort of disapproval that Delius might have known a decade earlier:

Here comes good-natured Harry, swift to learn,
Yet slow to study where stern memory rules;
With apprehension keen, he oft doth spurn
    The modes of Mathematics taught in schools.

Finally, even the idealistic George Schwarz, absorbed with preparations for the priesthood, did not escape the detached amusement of Ward, who peppered his limerick with allusions now lost to us:

What ailed old "Gunboats" through the passing hours,
That Knowledge left him often in the lurch?
Was too much "Mail" the cause, or "Rhyming" powers,
    Or mind ecstatic wrapped in mystic search?
Perhaps his "pedal weights" kept down his brains
    Or Muse unwilling caused him secret pains.

As school catalogues evidence, Frater Paul's teaching duties expanded steadily and, by 1895–96, he had become "Director of Music" and "Professor of History, Political Economy, Phonography and Mental Philosophy"—while continuing his studies for the priesthood.[19] From Father Benedict's diary entry of February 16, 1895, we learn of another of Ward's unsuspected talents: he initiated a course in "Architectural Drawing, the first in the history of St. Leo's."

"Phonography," as shorthand was then called, was a new business skill, but one already important to a commercial curriculum. In early 1893 Frater Paul completed a correspondence course with Pernin's Shorthand Institute in Detroit.[20] The Pernin system that Ward taught was a variant of a method invented by the French priest Abbé Émile Duployé and used in many Catholic institutions. (Pernin shorthand, in turn, would be superseded by the Pitman and Gregg systems, to which it bears no resemblance.[21])

A passage in Ward's hand, discovered in the monastery's archives, has remained to this day undecipherable, despite several shorthand experts' attempts to translate it. Appearing next to his certificate, the symbols may describe nothing more than Ward's relief at finishing the correspondence course. Or do they contain another secret message? The scribblings remain today as elusive as a tablet of ancient Sumerian.

Although classroom responsibilities left little time for entertainment and sports, life at St. Leo was not all arduous discipline and gloomy routine. Like

Thomas F. Ward's shorthand message.
(St. Leo Archives.)

the young Delius, Ward loved the water and enjoyed "bathing," as swimming was then called. Father Benedict noted on April 2 that Ward had built the new bathhouse for the 1892 swimming season. Frater Paul himself reported: "Nothing so acceptable has transpired since the opening of the school year as the privilege of bathing in Clear Lake, which was granted to the students April 6th." He enjoyed the merriment of his pupils who "so naturally and gleefully . . . take to the water."[22] Besides swimming, his cadets enthusiastically played "base ball" in the spring months.

The other monks also occasionally needed some worldly fun. Father Benedict informs us that on March 21, 1892, St. Benedict's Day, Father Charles, Father Roman, and Frater Paul (Ward) "entertained the cadets in the study hall with comic songs & stories." There were many other small pleasures. In May of 1894, Frater Dominic briefly abandoned his religious studies to catch a "13 1/4 trout in Lake Johnnie" (Lake Jovita); that June the monks and seminarians partook from a "32-gal. barrel of superb Eye-opener" donated to the Reverend Procurator by "Mr. I. Hopper."[23] And on Father Charles's thirty-second birthday, January 24, 1895, the Fathers "spent a happy free time in the company of Bohunkus Voelm and played checkers, cards, & poker with chips, which Father Prior recently bought for the Fathers' amusement." But, Father Roth confessed to his diary that day, the monks always played cards in "a moderate manner," their inclination now being more "towards billiards chiefly." As we might suspect, "Bohunkus Voelm" was one of his many code names for beer!

Privacy was rare in this closely knit community where thriftiness was prized. Even commonplace throwaway articles were useful to the whole group. Father Benedict's journal entry of February 23, 1895, describes how "the box in which our first piano came [was] all along used as a feed box in the

May 9th Bro. Charles Eckel, O.S.B., left for Maryhelp Abbey. May 11th Ascension.
Rev. Fr. Leo sang highmass at 7.00 during which Delaporte, Nordhaus, Brown and
Syd Einig made their First Holy Communion. Rev. Fr. Charles & Fr. James only
sang in the choir. — Benediction at 4.00 p.m. — Rev. F.F. Benedict & Leo took supper
at Cruss' (across the lake). May 16th the Fathers, Brothers and Students went
on an Excursion from St. Leo Station to St. Petersburg, Fla. The cadets held a Dress
Drill at the then only large Hotel front; returned at 9.00 p.m. Drizzly all day —
May 22nd Pentecost Monday. The whole house assisted at Sol. Highmass at San
Antonio. Afterwards they were all present at the Entertainment in the San Antonio
School Hall in honor of Rev. Fr. Roman — this being his nameday. May 30th This
is Memorial Day. Rev. Fr. Leo sang Requiem highmass at 7 o'clock. June 1st Cor-
pus Christi. Sol. highmass by Rev. Fr. Leo, Cel., Rev. Fr. Benedict Deac. & Rev. Fr. J.
Moore Subd. Afterwards Procession to three altars at College entrance, at Dr.
Corrigan's gate entrance — rather then on his grounds and in the Brothers', St.
Benedict's Convent, Chapel. The College Brass Band played during the Procession.
The players were Rev. Fr. Charles, (Rev. Fr. Roman), Fr. James & Fr. Paul. June 3.
Mr. Shadel of Sanford, Fla, & formerly of Latrobe, Pa., photographed at St. Leo's.
June 9th Feast of the Sacred Heart of Jesus. Rev. Fr. Charles Celebrant, Rev. Fr. Leo
Deacon, Rev. Fr. Benedict Subdeacon; the cadets received Hl. Com. in a body. June
14th Wednesday. Oral examinations of the classes were held daily, till Saturday
inclusive. June 19th Sing Rev. Wm. Kenny & Rev. Fr. Patrick Donlon, O.S.B., arrived.
June 20th Exhibition Day. Very Rev. Kenny, D.D., Celebrant, Rev. Fr. Patrick Deacon,
Rev. Fr. Benedict Subdeacon, Rev. Fr. Leo Master of Ceremonies, Rev. Fr. Roman, Fr. James
& Fr. Paul sang on the choir; afterwards Benediction. Commencement Exercises at 2.
30 p.m. — In his Address, Rev. Fr. Kenny spoke on Education: Book Learning, Education
of the Heart, Reviewed the Benedictine Order as a teacher, and mentioned State Education.
The Hall (Study Hall, northern part of second floor containing three double windows)
was crowded to its utmost capacity. In the evening the Fathers enjoyed "Pigs feet"
of which Fr. Kenny is very fond; but "Belni" failed to arrive again. (See
March 17th 1892 page 17.) On June 21st Rev. Fr. Director sent Bros. Andrew with
Rev. Fr. Kenny, Patrick & Benedict to St. Joseph's School Commencement. They
went out on the Buckboard! Took dinner at Mr. Charles Bartlo, they also
called on Mr. Jno. Klein who treated them with Strawberry wine. Both these
men are very respectable gentlemen. The following day the Fathers spent at
Father Roman's. — June 23d The Rev. visitors left via Dade City for Jax.
June 27th Rev. Fr. Director took his first bath in Clear Lake today with Rev.
Fr. Benedict, Fr. James and Geo. Schwarz, & vouched continuance thereof. He
kept his word faithfully. ░░░
June 28th Mr. Mortimer Murphy, a big fat man, procured particulars for a
U.S. National Biography from Rev. Fr. Charles. June 30th Rev. Fr. Patrick visited.
July 1st Rev. Fr. Director with Geo. Schwarz made & lined on both sides the new
road running from the college to the public road on the old college land.
The road was lined with Australian Oaks which froze in '94-'95. July 6th Rev. Fr. Char-
les left for Belmont, N.C. & since Bro. James Post for his home Mahonoy City, Penna.

A page from Father Benedict Roth's chronology. "June 1st Corpus Christi. . . . The College Brass Band played during the Procession. The players were Rev. Fr. Charles, (Rev. Fr. Roman), Fr. James & Fr. Paul [Ward]." (St. Leo Archives.)

stable and today Brother Leo, having made a smoke house of it, is smoking our recently butchered pork & he succeeded very well." Surely before the container met its humble destiny, the piano had been delivered over to Frater Paul for his music lessons.

One wonders how Frater Paul, with many practical and spiritual duties, could have had any time left over for music. And what did he expect to accomplish musically with a group of unenlightened cadets? Ward soon gathered a few private piano students, whom he taught twice weekly. This routine is, in fact, confirmed by the teaching schedule of Mrs. James Mooney, who took over Ward's four piano students for a short time in 1894, briefly attracting local attention as St. Leo's first woman teacher.[24] As a professional musician, Ward was required to provide music for holiday celebrations and feasts (Thanksgiving, Christmas, etc.), commencement exercises, and special religious occasions such as St. Benedict's Day. The college's catalogues clarify his responsibilities. He was expected to conduct the school orchestra and the newly founded St. Benedict's choir, whose "members endeavor[ed] to increase devotion and piety by providing suitable music at Divine services." Occasionally he directed the "St. Cecilia Quartette" in secular vocal music.[25]

Following in the Benedictines' tradition, several of Ward's monk colleagues at St. Leo were music lovers. When not pursuing his photography and architectural drawing, the Bavarian-born Frater James Shabaker taught violin, piano, and clarinet.[26] Arriving in 1893, Frater Louis Panoch—the recording secretary of the Order—was a proficient violinist who also found time to play first base on St. Leo's baseball team.[27] Probably the most gifted of Ward's companions, Frater Lawrence Wiegand organized and wrote plays for the school's first student theater group in 1893: the St. Lawrence Dramatic Association. Frater Lawrence, like Ward, was consumptive; he died at St. Leo in 1897 at the age of twenty-three.[28] Although it cannot be documented, Frater Paul may have provided the music for the theatrical organization. On January 6, 1893, before Frater Lawrence's arrival, Father Roth relates that the students performed "for the first time in the history of the College . . . [in] dialogues and recitations," with the accompaniment of a brass band and piano. Ward, with a Brooklyn background of similar entertainments, was very likely the organizer of this event. It should be noted that the theatrical tradition at St. Leo has continued from Frater Lawrence's day to the present. The school's most famous student was the actor Lee Marvin, who pursued acting and hell-raising in about equal measure before being expelled in 1942.

Frater Paul doubtless also befriended Father Roman Kirchner (1860–1920), the pastor of St. Anthony's Church in San Antonio just over the hill. Father Roman was a strong if difficult, stubborn, and uncooperative person, who constantly quarreled with Father Charles, but he was also a popular musician whose San Antonio Brass Band gave concerts of professional caliber.

With no other documentation, we must rely on St. Leo's annual commencement programs for information about the monastery's public music during the 1890s. St. Leo's graduation festivities attracted the attention of the highest Catholic officials in Florida. Bishop John Moore delivered the commencement addresses in 1894 and 1895. When, on June 18, 1894, the St. Leo "orchestra" (cadet Ollie J. Miller, piano; Frater Paul Ward, violin; Prior Charles, tenor horn; Rev. James, clarinet; and Frater Lawrence, cornet) performed "Battle Won," "Love's Confession," the galop "King of the Road," and other selections, Father Benedict exulted in his diary: "It was grand! And this was the best exhibition so far!"

What music might the good priest already have heard at St. Leo's graduation exercises? At the second annual commencement (June 16, 1892), Frater Paul, as pianist, kicked off the ceremonies with "Clickety Click,"[29] a lighthearted march composed by Fred T. Baker. Published in 1880 and dedicated to "Miss M. Kerr," Baker's march may have been one of Father Charles's favorites, used often to accompany the cadets as they proudly marched on stage to receive their diplomas.

Were one to find and examine other pieces played on that day, a persistent researcher, ferreting out Carl Bohm's "Market Maid" or Murphy's "Tampa Bay Hotel," would in all likelihood discover that these pieces, too, were average salon offerings of the period—like practically everything else on the school's graduation programs. There is, however, an exception to the norm. In his first public appearance at St. Leo, pianist Frater Paul performed one of his own pieces: "Waltz by Ward," subtitled "Full of Love." Unfortunately, we will never know how good Ward's waltz was, for all that survives is its enigmatic title. Full of what manner of love, we wonder, and love directed toward whom? Could the piece have been even remotely similar to Delius's music in style?

The *Florida Times-Union* reported on June 25, 1893, that the St. Leo orchestra's commencement music was "sweetly rendered . . . under the able direction of Fra[ter] Paul—formerly Professor Ward," the paper added for the benefit of its Jacksonville readers. Among the "sweetly rendered" pieces were "Ten-

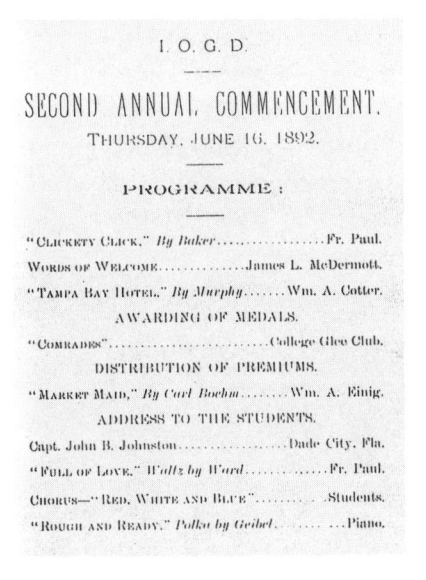

I. O. G. D.

SECOND ANNUAL COMMENCEMENT.

THURSDAY, JUNE 16, 1892.

PROGRAMME :

"CLICKETY CLICK." *By Baker* ....Fr. Paul.

WORDS OF WELCOME.............James L. McDermott.

"TAMPA BAY HOTEL." *By Murphy* ....Wm. A. Cotter.

AWARDING OF MEDALS.

"COMRADES"........................College Glee Club.

DISTRIBUTION OF PREMIUMS.

"MARKET MAID," *By Carl Boehm* ....Wm. A. Einig.

ADDRESS TO THE STUDENTS.

Capt. John B. Johnston................Dade City, Fla.

"FULL OF LOVE." *Waltz by Ward* ....Fr. Paul.

CHORUS—"RED, WHITE AND BLUE".........Students.

"ROUGH AND READY." *Polka by Geibel*........ ...Piano.

Fred T. Baker, "Clickety-Click" (1880). (Library of Congress.)

Second Annual Commencement Program, St. Leo Military College, June 16, 1892. (St. Leo Archives.)

der Flower," "Little Darling Dream of Mine," and "Home Sweet Home" (played by the orchestra), as well as the piano solos "Polka de la Reine" and "Loin du Bal," presumably performed and possibly composed by Frater Paul. An opening "Marche Militaire" by "Becker" and a closing "Slumber Polka" by the orchestra enlivened the ceremonies, at which Father William Kenny, Ward's former employer in Jacksonville, gave the commencement address.

Though the performer is not named, Ward must have been the pianist who performed Chopin's "Brilliant Variations" when degrees were conferred the next year on June 18, 1894. His love of Chopin has already been noted, and who at St. Leo but Ward could have executed Chopin's graceful but difficult *Variations Brillantes*, op. 12, on Ferdinand Hérold's "Je vends des scapulaires" (1833)? We can imagine that Chopin's youthful piece would have annoyed the brothers, who were forced to listen to a virtuoso piano work when attention was to have been focused on their cadets. On that day Ward shared pianistic honors with the already mentioned Ollie J. Miller, a Sanford native who performed "Thine Own" (composer unknown). We can be certain that the piece was more attuned to the audience's tastes.

The orchestra seems to have relied on a crowd-pleasing menu of senti-mental titles such as "Beautiful Isle of the Sea" (march), "Mollie Darling," "All in a Garden Fair" (waltz), and Foster's "Beautiful Dreamer" (serenade), all played during the 1895 commencement service. The German community's newspaper in San Antonio reported on similar pieces performed at the 1896 graduation, in which Frater Paul took part:

> The opening march was performed with mastery by the College Orches-tra. . . . A Quintet, "Klänge aus der Heimath" ["Sounds from the Home-land," Op. 31, by Joseph Gungl, 1810–1889], commanded the attention of those present and earned enthusiastic applause. . . . The students [sang] the pretty song "Home Sweet Home," in which—at the request of the President—those attending joined. . . . The festivities concluded with the rendering of "Ariel" [galop], by the College Orchestra.[30]

The level of public music at St. Leo seems commonplace for a community of scholars and intellectuals—even in the Florida backwoods. Ward probably had no time to compose anything other than the practical pieces required of him, like the "Waltz by Ward." Except for a tiny musical fragment, none of his music seems to have survived. In one of St. Leo's scrapbooks (beneath the shorthand message described above) can be found a four-measure passage in Thomas F. Ward's hand—a cadence of sweet chromatic inflection unmistak-ably reminiscent of Delius's style in the late 1880s, a musical mirror refract-ing the influence on (and perhaps of) Delius's own early style.

In contrast to the waywardness of Delius's earliest music, however, a dis-ciplined mind seems to control this music. Ward's strict two-part writing, above a chromatically descending bass line, accompanies the Latin words "*Tibi valedico; iam sis felix*" (I say to you, goodbye; I hope you are lucky from now on).[31] He specifies an exact tempo ("Tempo-Moderato. Quarter note = 76 m.m.") and provides the fingering for each note, albeit in the archaic nineteenth-century manner, with thumb designated by "x," forefinger by "1," and so on. This manner of fingering, common in French music, is per-haps further proof of Ward's study with the French-trained John Loretz in Brooklyn. The part-writing is smooth and the several musical suspensions suggest sadness or perhaps regret. This assured passage contrasts significantly with St. Leo's lackluster ceremonial music. If we could only discover an en-tire mass by Frater Paul in this confident flowing style! Like so much about Ward, however, the fragment remains part of a riddle, remote and beyond explanation.

Thomas Ward's musical cadence.
(St. Leo Archives.)

But what does the text of this mysterious musical cadence mean? Might it refer to its composer's hidden wish to leave the monastic way of life? Could it point to the composer's unhappiness? And to whom does Ward bid farewell and wish luck "from now on"? We must look more deeply into the religious way of life at St. Leo for answers.

↦ To enter into the monastic life, a monk must surrender his personality to the monastery and give up his own identity to contemplate the Divine. If he does not accomplish these goals, he will remain unhappy and unfulfilled. Ward's music and conduct at St. Leo suggest an inner experience apart from the other monks and potentially at odds with their aesthetic and religious way of life. His behavior at St. Leo reflects not so much the austere spiritual life within the monastery as the sensuous world outside—the world of Fritz Delius. As Ward had known at Solano Grove and as Percy Grainger observed much later, "To be with Delius was to feel oneself participating in a constant ritual celebrating enjoyment."[32] To live at peace among monks, he would have had to give up completely this worldly outlook.

The only photograph in which Thomas F. Ward can be identified with certainty is a St. Leo faculty portrait of June 1893. It shows a somewhat defiant-looking bearded man seated poised and seemingly confident at the right of Rev. Charles and the other faculty: Father James, Father Benedict, Father Louis, and Father Lawrence. If somewhat proud in demeanor, Frater Paul nevertheless appears to be an accepted member of the optimistic-looking leadership circle. In 1897, four years after this picture was taken, the monks listed Frater Paul's name in the faculty directory of the St. Leo catalogue of

1896–97 with an asterisk beside and the explanation: "died in course of the year."[33]

This blunt statement was the news Fritz Delius received when he briefly returned to Florida in that very year. Perhaps Ward was on Delius's mind that spring as he completed the elegiac second movement of his Piano Concerto in the seclusion of Solano Grove. Percy Grainger later observed that a "'darky' feeling is particularly noticeable in the slow movement and the beauty and poetry of this section alone is sufficient to immortalize the work."[34] William Henry Humiston, the American composer and program annotator for Grainger's New York performance in 1915, wrote that "the theme of the slow movement (and in fact most of the themes) was composed in Florida and breathes American Southern feeling. The glowing warmth and wistful sentiment of this movement are indeed typical of Delius himself, yet they also recall the emotional quality of America's two enthralling composers— Stephen Foster and Edward MacDowell."[35] The piece is imbued throughout with deep melancholy.

In 1917, twenty years after Delius returned to Europe, the monks published the old St. Leo faculty photograph during the twenty-fifth anniversary of the college. But they had clipped Ward out, as if he had never existed.[36] In falsely announcing to world that he had died, they unwittingly kindled the chain of rumors that Delius took back to Europe and inadvertently passed on to Philip Heseltine, Eric Fenby—and music history. Why did Frater Paul be-

The faculty of St. Leo Military College, June 1893. From left: Fr. James Shabaker, Fr. Benedict Roth, Fr. Charles Mohr, Fr. Louis Panoch, Fr. Lawrence Wiegand, Fr. Paul (Thomas F.) Ward. (St. Leo Archives.)

Frederick Delius, Piano Concerto in C Minor, Second Movement (1897, rev. 1907). Reduction for two pianos. (By permission of Boosey & Hawkes, Ltd.)

come "dead" in their minds, a nonperson who could still disturb their peace of mind a generation later? To answer this question, we must look at the hard religious journey upon which Frater Paul had embarked in 1891.

The road toward the priesthood can be difficult even under the best of conditions. As the Benedictines explained: "The candidate for the priesthood begins his monastic life after his second year of college. His philosophical and theological studies, which prepare him for the sacred ministry, are begun after he takes vows following a year's novitiate. Solemn Vows at the completion of the temporary Vows make his life and work a lifelong sacrifice to God."[37]

Ward did complete "his second year of college," finishing Second Theology in 1893. But from the outset he strayed from his path by absenting himself from the monastery without permission. In April 1893, with his preparatory religious studies ending, he notified Father Charles that he intended to leave St. Leo but, at Mohr's urging, agreed to remain until vacation time.[38] Apparently this crisis soon passed. With his novitiate approaching in 1894, he again abruptly announced his departure—for the third time according to Father Benedict's April 6 journal entry—but "finally decided to remain and reform." With time for vacillation rapidly ending, Frater Paul still could not make up his mind to take the next step toward ordination.

Finally, on June 25, 1894, in the company of young Dominic Schwarz (and another monk, Brother Leonard), Ward set out on the 540-mile journey north to North Carolina to begin his novitiate. At 7:15 A.M. on July 11, he began his vows of silence at Maryhelp Abbey under a new religious name: "Frater Peter."[39] He behaved well in the early months, for the St. Leo chapter minutes of October 7, 1894, recorded that "a vote was taken [at St. Leo], which resulted in the Acceptance of both" Schwarz and Ward as novitiates at Maryhelp Abbey.[40] It seems likely that at this juncture Ward intended never to return to Florida. In assuming a new religious name he was seemingly transferring his vows of stability from St. Leo to Belmont.

No abbey records survive concerning Brother Peter's residence in North Carolina, but the reason is easily apparent: midway through his novitiate, he abandoned Maryhelp Abbey and on January 15, 1894, suddenly reappeared at St. Leo to the astonishment of everyone—Father Benedict Roth, most of all. He had taken yet another religious name, Roth noted: "At Sext, at 6.25 a.m., there enters Ven. Fr. Placidus (Paul, Peter,—alias Thomas) Ward in his return from Maryhelp Abbey. It was a surprise. He looked real well & strong."

The old Abbey Cathedral, Maryhelp Abbey, ca. 1908. (Archives of Belmont Abbey, Belmont, N.C.)

He had indeed become Frater Placidus, a person in good health and, with the priesthood temporarily postponed, for the moment at peace with himself. In the one-hundred-year history of St. Leo Monastery, no other Benedictine monk has ever had more than one name.[41] Yet Thomas F. Ward had three! It cannot be accidental that his first (Paul) was the namesake of his baptismal church in Brooklyn, a place deeply symbolic of his identity. In contrast, the second (Peter) represented not a sudden revelation of faith, but an all-too-human temporary loss of it. It is perhaps coincidental that his first two names were those of the Brooklyn church (SS. Peter and Paul) where he had experienced his greatest musical successes. But what can be said about his final name, Placidus? Most likely it was given to him by Father Charles— now Prior Charles—in the hope that the confused, unhappy monk would find placidity, serenity, and peace of mind.

Whatever the reason, Prior Charles Mohr accepted Frater Placidus Ward back into the fold and forgave his transgressions. He did not want to lose one of his best teachers. To keep his restless monk occupied, he announced in July 1895 that Placidus Ward would hold summer classes "to lay a good foundation for the studies that [the students] are to pursue next year."[42] By summer's end, the monks made peace with Ward and unanimously voted, at Father Charles's proposal, to accept both "Ven. Frs. Placidus Ward and Dominic

Schwarz for Simple Vows."[43] All that remained before Ward's ordination was his taking of solemn vows, a step customarily made three years after simple vows but in special cases permitted after a shorter period. Ward's was indeed a special case.

Could anything prevent Placidus from attaining this goal? There was, I believe, a fundamental obstacle. Thomas F. Ward possessed a terrible secret that, though shared earlier with Delius, remained hidden from the monks: he was the illegitimate son of a priest. As a Jesuit priest explained to me, unless an individual has special dispensation, illegitimacy alone bars him from being ordained. And if he is also the son of a priest? With special permission from Bishop Moore and the Catholic Church (and with more determination and less pride), Ward might have entered the priesthood, on condition that he live a life of special penance. But the spiritual suffering and social penalties to pay within the monastery would have been enormous.[44] As the time for perpetual vows drew nearer, Frater Placidus, keeping his secret to himself, was about to break a basic law of the Church and commit a fundamental trespass that his conscience could not sustain.

Why had he chosen this life, and what had been his perhaps unconscious motivation? As Sister Mary Albert Lussier, archivist of the Sisters of St. Joseph in Florida, noted, Thomas Ward believed that his father, lacking self-discipline, had "ruined another's reputation, and rejected his son. . . . [Thomas] needed to achieve (or to fail also?) in a pattern where his father had failed."[45] Not many are given a chance to remedy another's deep transgression. In the celibate monastic life, Ward could set everything right between himself and both his earthly father and his heavenly Father. An orphan, he could make amends by embracing the religious family, accepting responsibility and discarding guilt, being faithful to the Mother of the Church. But he was also dangerously close to reenacting the past by deserting the Order, leaving his family, and reliving his father's experience. Rejected in real life by his father, Ward was in a situation where he could be rejected in religious life by the Benedictine's father-figure Prior Charles. He faced a psychological and spiritual dilemma.

Ward realized that he was temperamentally unfitted for the religious profession, that monastic life was unsuited to his basic nature. One of St. Leo's monks bluntly said: "For a strong independent personality, life can be miserable" in a monastic community.[46] As Sister Mary Albert described Ward's situation to me on December 11, 1986, a few months after my visit to St. Leo:

"A genuine vocation from God is necessary to survive the frictions in this special way of life." But to take simple vows and then abandon a position of trust, to leave a monastery without the order's permission, to violate vows of obedience—presented equally unacceptable alternatives. In those days, if a man entered and then deserted a monastery, he was known among the Irish as a "spoiled priest."[47] For Ward, this behavior would mean unthinkable failure and could be an enduring stain on the conscience of a deeply religious man now entering middle life.

Just before beginning his novitiate, on May 2, 1894, the day of the Vigil of the Ascension, Ward composed a poem entitled "The Request." It was his request to the Virgin Mary—a prayer that in her vigil before the cross the Holy Mother would not forget him:

> When, in the deep recesses of thy heart
> > Thou art communing with celestial powers,
> Let but a shadow of thy thought depart
> > For me, that I may wisely use my hours.
>
> Flowery soil may rest upon a rock;
> > Lives appearing gentle may be hard;
> Woman's prayers no spirit e'er may mock,
> > And men despairing, find them still their guard.
>
> He, that appeared when arisen to woman first,
> > To whom his mercy once had well been given,
> He, that His Mother kept from sin accurst,
> > Will hear thy prayers and bring my soul to Heaven.[48]

Frater Paul's private and revealing poem reflects a troubled past. It seems to be a prayer for his own mother, whom he defends for not having abandoned him, for keeping him "from sin accurst." Ward, I believe, must have been aware of her identity and fate. The verses are also a prayer for deliverance spoken by a man with an undisclosed past, whose life though "appearing gentle . . . may be hard," a confession from a man in spiritual conflict whose redemption resided in disciplined activity and in "wisely using his hours." Thomas Ward—alias Paul, Peter, Placidus—had long controlled his emotions, but by autumn 1896, five years after he arrived at St. Leo, he could no longer set them aside. The night had not gone and the dark shadows had not faded away. Instead, the hour of crisis had arrived.

Thomas F. Ward, 1893 (detail of photograph on page 96).

✦ Crisis: St. Leo and Tampa

"You can do nothing with an impossible subject."
—THOMAS F. WARD

On June 14, 1986, when Ward's presence at St. Leo Monastery was still unknown to anyone, Sister Mary Albert Lussier wrote to me about a Jesuit named Father Philip de Carriere, who in Florida's pioneer days encountered many people and "was back and forth wherever a few Catholics settled." She felt certain that at some point "Ward met with this wonderful missionary." Her intuition was soon proved correct, confirmed by documents at St. Leo that came to light shortly thereafter.

On June 22, 1896, ninety years before, Thomas F. Ward—Frater Placidus—entered into spiritual retreat with the Jesuits of Tampa, Florida. The little wooden Church of St. Louis at which he arrived was called the "Mother of Missions" because of the Society of Jesus's zealous missionary activities in wilderness Florida.[1] Its doors were always open to any monks from St. Leo in need of retreat. At St. Louis Church, Ward soon befriended the Rev. Philip de Carriere, S.J. (1825–1913), one of the most principled and compassionate priests in Florida's Catholic history. It was a meeting that would be especially propitious. In early summer 1896, Thomas F. Ward had finally come to the right place at the right time.

Philip de Carriere was born in 1825 in Toulouse, France, the scion of an aristocratic French family. Joining the Society of Jesus as a young man, he fled France during the Revolution of 1848, along with other Jesuit priests, and settled in the United States, where he became a distinguished teacher and scholar at Jesuit colleges in Spring Hill, Alabama, and New Orleans.

In 1888, Bishop Moore, in desperation in St. Augustine, invited the Jesuits in New Orleans to come and assist the Catholic Church in south Florida, where yellow fever epidemics had exacted a terrible toll among the Catholic

Father William J. Tyrrell,
S.J. (Courtesy Sacred Heart
Church, Tampa.)

Father Philip de Carriere, S.J.
(Loyola University Archives.)

population and had carried off three priests in Tampa alone. Father de Carriere, a master of many languages (including Spanish), had lived in the Caribbean and considered himself immune to the deadly fever. In 1888, age sixty-four, he arrived at St. Louis Church in the fever-ravaged seaport, where his ministrations to the sick soon took him, "regardless of infection, by boat and mule cart and on foot to the remotest areas" as an "Apostle of South Florida."[2]

When Father de Carriere died in Macon, Georgia, in his eighty-eighth year, on January 27, 1913, it was noted that he was "the soul of sincerity and honor. He feared no man." Like Thomas Ward, the priest "had strong, definite views, and he expressed them just as strongly, but with never-failing courtesy," according to the *Macon Daily Telegraph*'s obituary on the following morning. He also loved music and had discriminating tastes in art. On New Year's Day 1891, for instance, the *Tampa Daily News* described his singing at vespers that Christmas as "very artistic and pious." What was to be most important for Ward, de Carriere, while "severe to himself, abstemious almost to excess . . . was indulgent to others" and had "the gift of guiding choice souls in the arduous path of perfection."[3] With the lifelong habits of a scholar, Father de Carriere kept a meticulous diary of his experiences in Florida.

While on retreat, Ward met a second churchman who took an interest in his spiritual welfare: the Rev. William J. Tyrrell, S.J., pastor since 1892 of St. Louis Church. Born in Ireland in 1854, Father Tyrrell was an educator, a generous man "of keen vision and cheerful optimism," and a priest who "seemed to have a philosophy of life that steered him through the most difficult places in a most successful way."[4] Many years later, a Jesuit priest, Father T. J. S. McGrath, remembered that era in Tampa in a memoir of his friend published in the *Tampa Daily Times* on October 15, 1923: "*Erant gigantes in diebus illis*—there were giants in those days." Father Tyrrell, he recalled, had a secure vision of Tampa's bright future and possessed the "power of taking the situation of men, things and circumstances."[5] The beloved priest of the Church of the Sacred Heart lived to celebrate his golden jubilee in 1923 and died the following year, a venerated figure in a much changed Tampa.

Different as their outlooks were, the Tampa Jesuits and the monks to the north had established cordial relations during the 1890s, and religious officials routinely traveled back and forth between their two institutions. Placidus Ward's retreat, however, seemed unusually urgent, for his arrival in Tampa took some of the Jesuit fathers by surprise. He had hardly arrived when, citing bureaucratic problems at the monastery, Father Charles suddenly terminated his much-needed rest and summoned him back to St. Leo. In the privacy of his diary, Father de Carriere hinted at both Mohr's shortsighted impetuousness and Frater Placidus's decency when he described the episode as follows:

June 22, 1896: Father A. Fontan returns from St. Leo. He came late by the last train of [the] Florida Central of Peninsula RR, and was accompanied with Br. Placidus O.S.B. whom we accommodated the best way we could with a bed in the Monastery that was already overcrowded.

June 23: Frater Placidus begins a kind of spiritual exercise (more or less curtailed). That Retreat was given him by Father Ph. de Carriere (to a certain degree and according to the circumstances) which Venerabilis Frater Placidus had regulated beforehand with the Rt. Rev. Father Charles O.S.B.

June 27: In the morning, Ven. Frater Placidus returned to St. Leo where he had been called by telegrams in order to form the choir of the monastery of that place: *tres faceient capitulum*, [3 absolutely required] and he was the No. 3—absolutely required. I feel confident God blessed Ven. Fr. Placidus O.S.B.; *mihi constat* [it is evident to me] that Ven. Frater P. blessed our mon-

astery. . . . We gave him a warm hospitality & the place of honor in our Refectory to honor in his person St. Benedict and the RR. FF. [Right Reverend Fathers] of St. Leo.[6]

It appears harsh on Mohr's part that Ward's retreat—"a kind of spiritual exercise"—was "more or less curtailed" to five days for such a petty reason—to complete the quota of a choir. (Father de Carriere's use of the word "absolutely"—in Latin and English—to describe the prior's insistence, should not go unnoticed.)

Whatever his "place of honor" among the Tampa fathers, Frater Placidus's relationship with his fellow monks at St. Leo became intolerable in the following months. He became moody and uncommunicative, habitually staying out overnight—in total disregard of the monastery rules.[7] Symptoms of a nervous breakdown were present when the crisis reached its climax on October 20, 1896. On that Tuesday morning Thomas F. Ward abandoned the monastery, fled to the neighboring village of San Antonio, and found a place of refuge. His exact whereabouts during the next two days are unknown. Did he perhaps seek out Father Roman Kirchner, the other musical and clerical outsider in the religious community around St. Leo? This seems likely.

Hoping to find his way out of the morass, Ward dispatched several letters from San Antonio to Father Charles—emotional and disturbing letters, reflecting love-hate feelings toward the prior, showing determination to leave the order but still leaving the door slightly open for reacceptance by the monks. Counting on sympathy, he completely misjudged Father Charles's disposition and failed to heed his unyielding nature. He seemed unable to foresee that his actions—even his attempts to *explain* his actions—would only further infuriate and alienate Charles Mohr. Why did he not realize the jeopardy of his situation? Of the three simple vows taken with the Benedictines, he had broken the first, the Vow of Stability, by fleeing to San Antonio; the second, the Conversion of Life, by continuing his secular habits; and (by disobeying his prior) was about to break the third and most important: the Vow of Obedience. He had placed himself in a position to be excommunicated from the Catholic Church.

From San Antonio, Ward summoned his friend and fellow musician Father James Shabaker and urged him to go back to the monastery and ask Father Charles to come to San Antonio to talk things out. Perhaps it was finally time to disclose his secret to the brothers. But Father James, anxious to avoid his prior's wrath, failed to deliver any message. What Ward did not

know was that Father Charles had not the least intention of going to San Antonio. He had already given up on his impossible subject.

When Mohr failed to appear the next day, Placidus Ward penned a letter into which he poured his despondency, uncertainty, and self-reproach. One of only four original letters in Thomas Ward's hand known to exist, it is here quoted in full:

San Antonio, Oct. 21, 1896

Rt. Rev. F. Charles, O.S.B.

Dear Father Charles,

When I left St. Leo's Yesterday morning, I had no intention of not returning. Since then I have concluded that it would [be] better if I did not return. No one at the College is in any way responsible for this conclusion.

If you had had any inkling of my decision, you *might* have satisfied *my request, made through Father James yesterday* afternoon. I say *might* instead of *would*, because I am not as sure about your desire to have me remain: for I have certainly been an unsatisfactory subject. But in either case the result would have been the same: I have no vocation, and I must be released.

I shall never return to St. Leo's again, even if you are unwilling to release me, or to send the few things mentioned in the enclosed list, which I ask for, because I need them. Father Benedict may put them together, if he is willing, as he is so careful, that I know he will forget nothing. Any one—Grimm for instance—can finish that ~~Architectural~~ Drawing, which I left incomplete in the room over the Post Office; it needs no further ruling, only free-hand and the lettering.

Besides the articles mentioned, will you send me enough to pay my fare to Tampa? I wish to leave today.

You deserve a better acknowledgement of your patience with me than this sudden departure: but you can do nothing with an impossible subject. I thank you for your kindness throughout, which I am sure would have been more marked and unremitting had I been better disposed and more regular.

> With the highest respect and most sincere affection,
> Believe me Yours Truly,
> (Frater Placidus) Thomas F. Ward[8]

Frater Placidus's name remained hesitatingly in parentheses as Thomas F. Ward's resurfaced for the first time in five years. Though presenting a negative self-portrait with little self-esteem, Frater Placidus did not deny himself gentle quips at both the "careful" Father Benedict and his less-than-brilliant architectural student John L. Grimm, who, according to the school catalogue for that year, won "Premiums for Drawing and Elocution." That he maintained an ironic sense of humor in his stressful situation shows a most appealing human trait in Placidus/Ward.

In a separate letter ("the enclosed list") to Benedict Roth, Frater Placidus requested the things he would need outside the religious community:

Dear Father Benedict, O.S.B.,

Please send the following today to San Antonio:
2 suits inside clothing
3 pair socks
some red & white handkerchiefs
2 pair cuffs (in my desk are a pair of sleeve buttons (gold) and a pair of cuff buttons/please send them with the cuffs.)
2 white shirts
some linen (not clerical) collars, size 15
a necktie
the pair of shoes under the bed
the black pair of trousers behind the door
I suppose F[ather] C[harles] will need the overcoat.
My razor is in the wash-stand drawer. Send me my comb and brush, and toothbrush. also blacking brush, and the clothes-brush and anything else you think I may have forgotten that will be necessary.

Yours truly, Fr[ater] Pl[acidus]

Please pack these in a satchel and send [them] to San Antonio.[9]

The hastily improvised list verifies that Ward's flight to San Antonio was, as his letter to Father Charles stated, spontaneous and unplanned, in other words, that Frater Placidus "had no intention of not returning."

As might be expected, Father Charles was offended by the admonitory tone of Ward's letter. He underlined in blue crayon Ward's request to see him

and, with a pointed barb at Father James's failure of nerve, sent the letter to be filed under "Ward" with an imperious note to the files: "Fr. James failed to bring me the message. At any rate I would not have gone to see him anyhow. I am more than glad to be rid of him. For two weeks before leaving he did not speak to anybody. C[harles]."[10]

To be fair to Father Charles and the other brothers, they had many good reasons to desire to rid themselves of a monk whose neurotic behavior they had tolerated for half a decade. Ward's individualism and many eccentricities revealed what is not uncommon in monastic life: "a man who is not at peace with himself necessarily projects his interior fighting into the society of those he lives with, and spreads a contagion of conflict around him."[11] Father Charles surely saw it as his duty to prevent any further spread of a contagion of conflict among those in his charge.

In the aftermath of Ward's actions, the monks convened hurriedly to deal with the sudden disorder within their community. In chapter minutes bearing the date of Ward's own letter (October 21), they quickly (but temporarily, as we shall later see) agreed to Placidus's request to be released from his simple vows because "he has no vocation in the religious life. The aforesaid letter is kept on file. Habitual disregard of the rules of the house and incompatibility of temperament urged the Rev. Chapter to grant his request."[12]

Ward, as he honestly and painfully acknowledged, truly had "no vocation," at least not in the strict monastic sense of unreservedly embracing solitude. And he probably neither gave to nor received much affection from his fellow monks. Thomas Merton has described this difficult predicament and its perils:

> To live alone with God, [an individual] must really be able to live *alone*. You cannot live alone if you cannot stand loneliness. And you cannot stand loneliness if your desire for "solitude" is built on frustrated need for human affection. To put it in plain language, it is hopeless to try to live your life in a cloister if you are going to eat your heart out thinking that nobody loves you. You have to be able to disregard that whole issue, and simply love the whole world in God, embracing all your brethren in that same pure love, without seeking signs of affection from them and without caring whether or not you ever get any. If you think this is very easy, I assure you that you are mistaken.[13]

Perhaps Ward still needed his fellow monks' affection, but receiving their negative decision via a monk-courier in San Antonio, he could now comprehend how thoroughly persona non grata he had become. Had he known that Father Charles would not meet him under any circumstance, he might not have composed his second letter of that day in the manner that he did, dropping his religious name and adopting a proud, elegantly impersonal style. There was now no going back:

San Antonio, Fla.

Oct. 21, 1896

Dear Father Charles,

I have the greatest respect and affection for the Fathers, but I do not propose to call again at St. Leo's. It will not be necessary for me to pass by the College in going to Tampa, as I may go via St. Petersburg.

There is no objection on my part to facing you, or to letting my departure be known. What you have foreseen had its origin yesterday after I left St. Leo's College.

I am very much obliged to you for releasing me. My determination was taken in any event.

If you can not have my satchel packed for me, I shall go to Tampa as I am, even if I have to walk there.

With much respect, I remain yours truly,

Thomas F. Ward[14]

Though he still held out the possibility of "facing" the prior, Ward surely guessed by now that Father Charles would not reply to this defiant communication. But he now introduced a puzzle. What had Father Charles "foreseen" that "had its origin yesterday," as Ward enigmatically phrased it? This cannot refer to his decision to leave St. Leo, for that possibility had originated not the previous day but years before, according to Father Roth. And surely, as a busy administrator, Father Charles did not "foresee" being left in the lurch in the midst of a school semester, with courses to be taught and musical-liturgical duties to be fulfilled. In the prior's eyes that would be a despicable abnegation of responsibility. The only certainty that might have been "foreseen" from Ward's behavior was, in fact, Father Charles's vengeful wrath. Perhaps we can conclude that he was referring to something vaguely scandalous, an incident of some sort involving a third party. Perhaps there

The Orange Grove Hotel, Tampa. (Courtesy Anthony P. Pizzo.)

had been a romantic entanglement with a woman in the town—he had, after all, been staying out nights—or maybe an incident with a fellow cleric. Such things were not unknown in cloistered communities. I will confess that for a long time I was inclined to believe in Ward's affair of the heart—if Delius had had his Florida sweetheart, why not Ward?—and I spent much time trying to determine who this woman in the San Antonio area might have been. But in the end, tempting as it was to imagine a romantic scenario, there simply was no evidence for it. It must have been as the monks so detachedly observed: Frater Placidus had "no vocation in the religious life." He was not fit to be a monk or priest, either temperamentally, as they knew, or spiritually, as he knew. Yet the tantalizing sentence remains. What had Father Charles foreseen, and why did it have its origin so suddenly on that fateful Tuesday? What crucial piece of the puzzle is missing?

The matter of Frater Placidus was finished, at least for the time being. Father Benedict noted dryly in his diary on October 21 how the monks dealt with him that day: "A trunk, all of his clothing and ten dollars were sent to him and he never did return; left for Tampa."

Two days later Thomas F. Ward took rooms in one of Tampa's oldest hotels, the Orange Grove, at the corner of Madison and East Streets in the heart of West Florida's commercial center. Sidney Lanier, visiting Tampa twenty

years earlier, had been delighted with the "large three-story house with many old nooks and corners, although clean and comfortable in appearance, and surrounded by orange trees in full fruit." Ward was not the first musician to enjoy the languorous atmosphere of the Orange Grove. Visiting Tampa shortly after the Civil War, J. A. Butterfield composed his famous ballad "When You and I Were Young, Maggie" at the hotel.[15]

In the hot bustling port, Ward must have found the Orange Grove Hotel's relaxed ambience a universe removed from St. Leo's tensions. But he had little time for its comforts. Before he could resume his secular life in good religious conscience, one matter needed to be resolved. He immediately wrote to Father Charles:

Tampa, Fla., Oct. 23, 1896.

Rt. Rev. F. Charles, O.S.B.

Dear Father Charles,

Will you kindly send me, at once, a Canonical complete dispensation from my vows and from every obligation that may bind me to the order of St. Benedict?

I am at present stopping at the Orange Grove Hotel, but I do not wish you to address your letter there. I would prefer that you address me—

Thos. F. Ward,

c/o Fr. De Carriere Tampa

With the best dispositions towards you personally and towards the Benedictine Order as a body,

I remain,

Yours truly,

Thomas F. Ward[16]

The urbane inflection of this letter must have been particularly galling to Father Charles, for he vowed never again to communicate with Ward. He now wanted him, in fact, out of the State of Florida and excommunicated from the Catholic Church. It did not matter whether his former subject was now "in care of" Father de Carriere. In the prior's mind Ward was dead, banished from the affairs of the righteous.

The former Paul/Peter/Placidus was unfit even to receive his daily correspondence. By coincidence, a postcard from Mary Ward arrived at St. Leo only weeks after her brother's precipitous departure. Addressed to the gen-

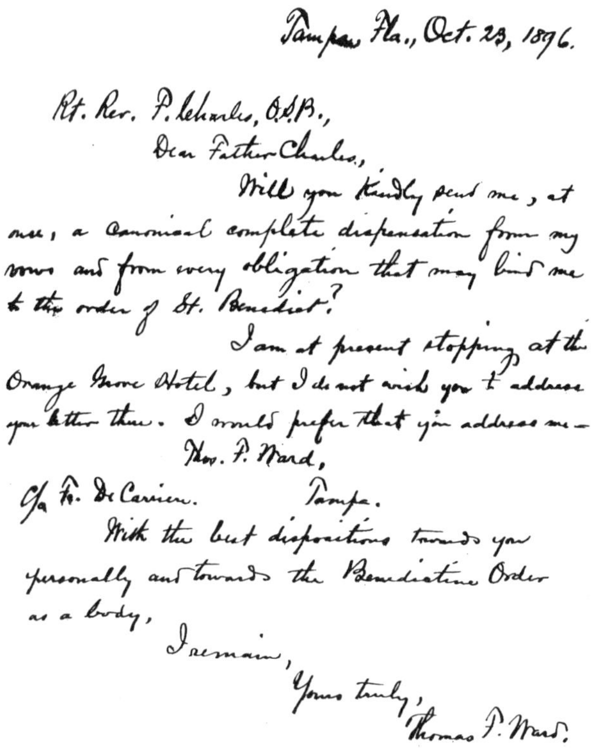

[handwritten letter]

Tampa Fla., Oct. 23, 1896.

Rt. Rev. P. Cehmlis, O.S.B.,
　　　Dear Father Charles,,
　　　　　　Will you kindly send me, at once, a Canonical complete dispensation from my vows and from every obligation that may bind me to the order of St. Benedict?
　　　　　　I am at present stopping at the Orange Grove Hotel, but I do not wish you to address your letter there. I would prefer that you address me —
　　　　　　　　Thos. F. Ward,
C/o Fr. De Carrier.　　　Tampa.
　　　　　　With the best dispositions towards you personally and towards the Benedictine Order as a body,
　　　　　　　　I remain,
　　　　　　　　　　Yours truly,
　　　　　　　　　　　Thomas F. Ward.

Letter from Thomas F. Ward to Father Charles Mohr, October 23, 1896. (St. Leo Archives.)

eral postmaster of St. Augustine, she obviously had not heard from Thomas in six years and had no inkling of his religious vocation:

Nov. 13th, 1896

Dear Sir!

Will you kindly give me the address of Mr. Thomas F. Ward (Musician). I am his sister and he is wanted on business of importance. If you know his address will you please send it right away to

　　　　　Miss Mary F. Ward
　　　　　St. Joseph's Convent
　　　　　Willoughby & Sumner Aves.
　　　　　Brooklyn N. Y.

And oblige yours very respectfully

　　　　　M. F. Ward[17]

The monks simply placed her entreaty in a scrapbook, since its subject was no longer considered alive.

Whatever required his immediate presence in Brooklyn, Ward never learned about it. Perhaps "the business of importance" concerned his real mother's estate, or perhaps his sister wanted to let him know that she was gravely ill with the cancer that would soon kill her. After the mysterious postcard, Mary Ward is never heard from again. Catholic newspaper reports show her to have been a gifted student, adept at music and recitation, and singled out for her "good conduct and proficiency" while at St. James Female School, an institution run by the Sisters of St. Joseph.[18] At the Brooklyn Lyceum in July 1875, the seventeen-year-old orphan participated in a religious play, "The Voyage of Life," a drama that, as the *Catholic Review* of July 17 related, "closed with a magnificent tableau, in which was displayed the rejoicing there is in heaven over the return of the sinner." Becoming a house servant, she kept her ties to St. Joseph's Orphanage Asylum and Convent and to the Sisters of Charity who had raised her. A resident in Brooklyn Heights (160 Joralemon Street) as the century turned, she died at St. Peter's Hospital, an "old maid," in her early forties.

❖ In Tampa in August 1986, the trail of Thomas F. Ward suddenly came to an end. No amount of local investigation produced a clue as to what happened to him after he had arrived at the Orange Grove Hotel ninety years earlier and sought out Rev. Philip de Carriere. The once famous hotel had been demolished decades ago. At the Sacred Heart Church, I found that all documents of St. Louis Church (including de Carriere's daybooks) had long since been removed to the Jesuits' archives in Grand Coteau, Louisiana, at the western edge of the great Achafalaya swamp. When I contacted Father Thomas Clancy, archivist of the New Orleans Province of the Society of Jesus, he graciously invited me to meet him in Grand Coteau, whenever he could schedule the 150-mile trip from Loyola University. But, in a letter of September 27, he cautioned that I would almost certainly find nothing in these books but reports of the routine comings and goings of Jesuits in the old days. If I wanted to grasp at straws, I was more than welcome to visit.

When in late October I drove up to the old retreat of Grand Coteau on a lovely Indian summer evening, I was welcomed by the Jesuit monks, provided with a cozy room, and served good Cajun food. The next morning, Father Clancy placed before me two ancient leather-bound volumes filled

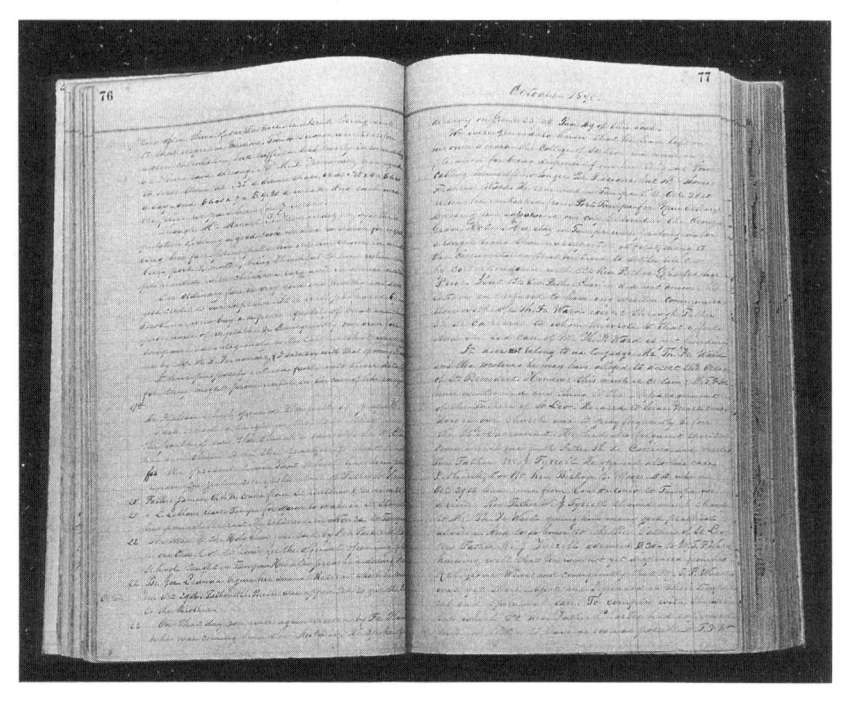

Father Philip de Carriere's house diary of St. Louis Church, Tampa, October 1896. (Photo by Sabine Matthes, orginal in Loyola University Archives.)

with Father de Carriere's meticulous ink script. They were the only manuscripts that might explain Ward's disappearance from Florida.

The mystery of Thomas F. Ward once again began to unfold. Over the abyss of time, Father de Carriere himself seemed at that moment to be telling me the story of the unhappy, failed cleric. He began his narrative on October 22, 1896, the day before Ward's last letter to Father Charles, and painted a portrait not of a nonchalant letter writer, but of a soul in distress:

October 22 [1896]. On that day we were again visited by Fr. Placidus who was coming from San Antonio. We spoke of him already on June 23, [18]96 Page 49 of this book.

We were grieved to know that he had left on his own accord the College of St. Leo and made an application for being dispensed from his Religious Vows, calling himself no longer Br. Placidus but Mr. Thomas Francis Ward. He remained in Tampa till Oct 31st when he embarked from Port Tampa for New Orleans. During his sojourn in our city he lived in the Orange Grove Hotel. His stay in Tampa was prolonged for a longer time

than was expected at first, owing to the circumstance that he tried to settle his case by correspondence with Rt. Rev. Father Charles his Prior. But Rt. Rev. Father Charles did not answer his letters and refused to have any written communication with Mr. Th. Fr. Ward except through Father Ph. de Carriere to whom he wrote to that effect. And the sad case of Mr. Th. Fr. Ward is yet pending.

It does not belong to us to judge Mr. Th. Fr. Ward and the motives he may have alleged to desert the order of St. Benedict. However this much is certain: Mr. T. F. W. never mentioned anything to the disparagement of the Fathers of St. Leo. He used to hear mass every day in our Church and to pray frequently before the B[lesse]d. Sacrament. He had also frequent spiritual communications with Father Ph. de Carriere and visited Rev. Father W. J. Tyrrell. He opened also his case, I think, to Rt. Rev. Bishop J. Moore D.D. who on Oct 29th had come from San Antonio to Tampa for a visit. Rev. Father W. J. Tyrrell showed much charity to Mr. Th. Fr. Ward giving him many good practical advices. And to do honor to the Rev. Fathers of St. Leo, Rev. Father W. J. Tyrrell advanced $30 to Mr. T. F. Ward knowing well that he was not yet dispensed from his Religious Vows and consequently that Mr. T. F. Ward was yet their subject and depended on their temporal and spiritual care. To comply with the desires which Rt. Rev. Father Charles had expressed him by letter to have as soon as possible Mr. T. F. W. out of the State of Fla without however sending him the money to travel, Rev. Father W. J. Tyrrell directed me to buy [for] Mr. Th. F. Ward a passage ticket for New Orleans, leaving him the change of a few dollars that he might use for his first necessary expenses in that city.

I regret to say that we have not yet heard of the arrival of Mr. Th. F. Ward in N.O. Neither do we know the direction to which we must send him his correspondence.[19]

We might note that Father de Carriere's narrative (quoted in its entirety) forms the most extensive account of any visitor to his church during his fourteen years in Tampa. On October 31, he made one further brief diary entry indicating that Thomas Ward had sailed from Tampa for New Orleans and reiterating that "$30—were advanced him by Rev. Father W. J. Tyrrell to pay for his passage trip, etc. etc." But after that date he never mentions his name again in his journal.

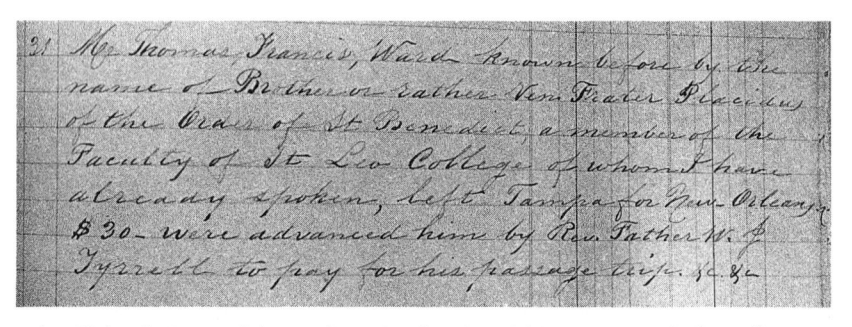

Father Philip de Carriere's house diary, October 31, 1896, containing the last reference to Thomas F. Ward. (Photo by Sabine Matthes.)

It was an unhappy leave-taking for one who had come to the South with high expectations more than twelve years earlier. Ward had little to show for an investment of much time in many parts of Florida. In leaving St. Leo, he had not asked Benedict Roth to bring music manuscripts to San Antonio; he seemed to be leaving his identity as a composer behind in Florida. It was time for a new beginning.

At the moment Ward was embarking, Florida was also on the mind of Fritz Delius, who planned to sail for America in just over two months. Delius had already composed his opera *Koanga* and was then working on his Danish songs with orchestral accompaniment.[20] One song, "Red Roses," alludes to time poorly invested—in Delius's case, in a pursuit of physical pleasure that would prove disastrous:

> Through long, long years we must atone,
> For what was a trifling pleasure;
> And what we dismiss with a careless smile,
> We cannot recall by long weeping
> For sorrows grow, and hot tears flow
> From red, red roses. (J. P. Jacobsen)

If Ward, too, had regrets about the past, he never revealed them. Father de Carriere's description of a man alone at the St. Louis Church altar is what remains as the end of Ward's Florida experience. The two Jesuit priests had given him spiritual support, and Bishop Moore seems to have traveled from St. Leo to Tampa to counsel a friend of ten years. It can hardly be a coincidence that both Father Tyrrell and Bishop Moore were down in the port of

Tampa (near the waterfront) the day before Ward sailed—"visiting the church interests there," according to the *Tampa Morning Tribune* of October 31.

At 8:00 P.M., Saturday, October 31, 1896, the steamship *Florida*, with Thomas F. Ward aboard, sailed out of Port Tampa on schedule, due to arrive in Mobile early on November 2, where connecting rail transportation would shorten the journey to the Crescent City. Florida was now in his past.[21]

Whatever Ward confessed to Father de Carriere in the St. Louis Church, disclosures so compelling that he would agree to leave Florida at the demand of St. Leo's monks, all these things went with Father de Carriere to the grave— as was appropriate. It was not his duty to pronounce judgment on Thomas Ward or on the motives for which "he may have alleged to desert the order of St. Benedict"—a strong word, "desert," carefully chosen by a concerned priest. But Father de Carriere did not forget him. "The sad case of Mr. Th. Fr. Ward" was, as the good priest reflected, "yet pending."

St. Louis Church, with the Sacred Heart Church under construction in the background, ca. 1905. (Courtesy Sacred Heart Church, Tampa.)

The altar of St. Louis Church, Tampa. (Courtesy Sacred Heart Church, Tampa.)

⤞ Louisiana and Texas

"Prudence directed him to act as he did in all things."
—FATHER PHILIP DE CARRIERE

On October 31, 1986, Halloween Day, I found myself in the French Quarter of New Orleans, by a strange coincidence ninety years to the day that Thomas F. Ward had sailed from Florida. He had arrived by train in New Orleans late on All Souls' Day, November 2, 1896, the eve of William McKinley's election to the presidency. With money left over from the thirty dollars Father Tyrrell had given him, Ward could have enjoyed the irony of Sidney Grundy's play *Sowing the Wind*, a drama about an orphan, Rosamund, whose "birth is enveloped in mystery" and who is "thrown upon the world from babyhood, without lawful parents, growing up a concert singer in the great city of London and winning the highest triumphs of her profession," announced the *New Orleans Daily Picayune* of November 1. It was the rage of the *Vieux Carré.*

Wandering around the city in search of clues, I found no evidence of his presence in Archdiocese and Jesuit records. Despite his penchant for fine hotels (as in Tampa), he was not to be discovered among the newspapers' daily hotel arrivals or, should circumstances have proven gloomier, in the rosters of Louisiana's sanitariums, mental institutions, and charitable organizations—all buried in the 1900 federal census. Indexed cemetery records for all Louisiana's parishes offered not a single clue. Where had he gone?

With only a few dollars to his name, Ward needed immediate employment. In addition to his French, he had probably acquired a passable knowledge of German among the emigrants of St. Leo and San Antonio. Perhaps he placed the following advertisement in the *Daily Picayune* of November 29 and December 6:

French, German and music;
easy methods; prices moderate;
331 Royal

But this was a thin lead, and no Thomas Ward was to be found at that address in city directories or in the 1900 census. Had he changed his name to begin a new life completely? That did not seem at all in character, given the bold use of his full name in his letters to Father Charles. The trail had once more ended.

I began to doubt whether Thomas Ward had ever arrived in New Orleans and, remembering William Cowper's religious poem "The Castaway," I tried not to believe the possibility of self-destruction that is suggested in its despairing lines:

Obscurest night involved the sky,
The Atlantic billows roared,
When such a destined wretch as I,
Washed headlong from on board,
Of friends, of hope, of all bereft,
His floating home forever left.

Returning to New York I learned that a Thomas F. Ward of New York had indeed committed suicide—but in the New Orleans City Park in 1907. I eventually traced this unfortunate individual—described by the *Picayune* of March 22, 1907, as an "insane New York lawyer . . . moody and taciturn but withal a gentleman in his manners and actions"—to Little Falls, New York, and verified that he was someone else. Whereas my confidence in Ward's stability sometimes wavered, Sister Mary Albert never doubted his spiritual strength and wrote to me confidently on December 11, 1986: "Whatever the crisis, our Thomas was a survivor. His health permitting, he would have managed, for I feel confident that he was distraught, not disoriented. Father de Carriere observed that the poor man was not alienated from the dear Lord, the Man of Sorrows, who always understands our human nature. . . . We are not at the end of our story."

Nineteen-eighty-seven passed with no further word on our Thomas F. Ward's whereabouts. A search through the sound index ("soundex") of the U.S. Census of 1900 revealed hundreds of "Thomas Wards" and dozens of "Thomas F. Wards" throughout the country, but not the erstwhile monk.

A most promising clue led me to a Professor Tom Ward (1857–1928) of Syracuse, a prominent director of choral music festivals in New York State for thirty years.[1] It was no surprise to discover that the Thomas F. Ward never held such a post in musical officialdom.

Then, at the beginning of 1988, Father Henry Riffle, on a brief return to St. Leo Monastery, located documents about Ward in the abbey archives that suddenly threw new light on Frater Placidus's predicament in late 1896. Father Riffle generously and selflessly made them available to me. It now became apparent that through Father de Carriere, Ward was determinedly continuing his efforts to obtain a formal dispensation from the Benedictines. On Ward's departure, Father Charles immediately wrote to Leo Haid, the Abbot Vicar Apostolate of Maryhelp Abbey, and inquired what should be done with Frater Placidus's case. Father Charles must have more than once urged strong action, for Abbot Haid acknowledged receipt of his "letters" and on November 2, 1897, pronounced the worst possible sentence, outlining in detail the canonical procedures involved:

> Thom. Ward is excommunicated by leaving your Monastery & has subjected himself to every censure of the church. . . . There is no question of Dispensation in reference to his Vows. . . . There is *materia gravis & sufficiens* [a matter grave and sufficient] for a formal expulsion from the Order. . . .
>
> I [will] write out the Formula which has to be signed by yourself and [the] Archabbot. One of these formulas you send then to Mr. Ward. The other you retain in your archive. This is all that need[s] to be done, then "Causa Finita est" [The case is finished].[2]

Less than two weeks after his escape to Tampa, Ward's situation had deteriorated alarmingly.

The new documentation at St. Leo now pointed directly to Ward's new (and improbable) location: "P.O. Box 54, Shreveport, La." As I soon discovered, he arrived in Louisiana's northwestern river port on January 6, 1897, after a two-month stay in New Orleans, and registered at the City Hotel (217 Milam Street near the Red River) as "Thomas F. Ward, New Orleans," as the *Shreveport Times*'s "Hotel Arrivals" column mentioned the next morning. But why, I now wondered, had he left the cosmopolitan Catholic city of New Orleans to journey to a primitive Protestant river town, 328 miles away by rail? At that time Shreveport was a busy port of around sixteen thousand people, just beginning to prosper from its growing logging and cotton in-

dustries.[3] It seemed an inhospitable place for a Catholic musician to make a new start in life.

Reaching Shreveport at the beginning of a record cold spell, Ward spent a desolate January 1897 preoccupied with his position vis-à-vis the Church. (In all likelihood he was unaware that he was being excommunicated.) One month after his arrival, he wrote a lengthy letter to Father de Carriere—his last known communication—which the priest copied "faithfully in its entirety" and forwarded to Father Charles. From its context we learn that de Carriere had been working patiently as an intermediary to establish peace between Charles Mohr and Thomas Ward and to bring this matter to a harmonious close. Ward's letter, wrote de Carriere, "speaks for itself and speaks well. Deo Gratias":

P.O. Box 54
Shreveport, La.
Feb. 5, 1897

Dear F[ather] de C[arriere].

Your letter of Jan. 30 and the Registry Return Receipt for the last letter I sent you were both rec'd by me together.

From the letter of Father Charles O.S.B., a copy of which you sent me, I infer that Father Charles has not yet rec'd the papers concerning my Absolution, etc.

In answer to the following extract from your letter, "I would like only a word or two from you to and by me for Rt. Rev. Fr. Charles that I might smooth your relation," I write the following:

As in all reason and justice I should be[,] I am grateful to Father Charles for his continued interest in my welfare; and I have likewise a great reverence and respect for him and the Fathers associated with him in his work of St. Leo.

That he may have evidence of my gratitude and affection, I propose, commencing this month to send him ten dollars every month, as long as I live and have employment: This will help to pay something towards my indebtedness to him.

In case he should be unwilling to accept any money from me beyond the thirty dollars advanced through Fr. Tyrrell S.J., I shall continue to send the same as a contribution to the Scholarship Fund, which he is trying to raise for St. Leo's.

Perhaps it will give you pleasure to see, by this proposition, that I am as kindly disposed to Father Charles as you could wish.

You will help, I think, to adjust our relations to each other, by assuring him that my departure from St. Leo, even as to the manner of it, was a question of Conscience with me, and I know that Father Charles is too true a Christian, to say nothing of his being too zealous a priest, to wish that I had acted otherwise.

Even if he should see fit to bar me altogether from his correspondence, I shall alter none of the feelings of gratitude and respect which I continue to entertain for him. He has seen too many instances of a headstrong, quarrelsome, faultfinding disposition on my part, to allow him to credit me with an affectionate disposition towards him: but, I think I love him as I know I once did, and that the feelings will be certain when he has assured me of his forgiveness for the past and his good will towards me for the future.

> Most respectfully & affectionately yours,
> Thomas Fr. Ward[4]

Texas Street, Shreveport, Louisiana, ca. 1898. (Archives of Louisiana State University in Shreveport.)

Immediately copying out Ward's letter for Father Charles on February 9, Father de Carriere paused to comment that he would later explain one paragraph (emphasized above):

> The extraordinary circumstances into which Mr. Thomas Francis Ward was then situated were such, though unknown to others, but well known to him, that Prudence directed him to act as he did in all things, in spite of unfavorable judgments of others, even of his own Superiors, judgments and their consequences which his *formata conscientia* obliged him to accept to that time God would appoint for his personal justification relatively to his decision—So much is certain.
>
> Assuming with good knowledge of those circumstances the responsibility of the opinions I've expressed[,] I rejoice more & more for the good turn that this unfortunate case is taking. I doubt not Rt. Rev. & dear Father that your Reverence and your saintly community will also rejoice with me.
>
> I must add to the good record of Mr. Th. F. W. that when in Tampa he entered no complaints against any of you but spoke favorably of all.
>
> Very respectfully and devotedly yours in X,
>
> Rev. Ph. De Carriere, S.J.[5]

From confessions (his "good knowledge"), Father de Carriere alone knew what had made Ward desert the monastery; he understood that Ward's illegitimacy (his "extraordinary circumstances . . . unknown to others") was a private spiritual matter, best left with his religious conscience. There were grounds for forgiveness in Ward's exercise of the cardinal virtue "prudence."

Ward's last known letter reveals much about his character and circumstances. He was a generous person with a forgiving nature who felt morally obliged to repay his debts. He had found steady employment with decent pay. If not, how could he offer to begin immediately repaying his debt and to contribute to St. Leo's scholarship fund for "as long as I live and have employment"? Ten dollars monthly was a substantial sum in 1897. He had found some measure of emotional stability and mental peace. Leaving the religious vocation, he had, ironically, at last become "Placidus."

Father Charles marked de Carriere's "explanation" in pencil and added a note: "keep with W.'s papers." We must conclude that Father de Carriere eventually persuaded Mohr that his action against Ward was morally wrong and not in St. Leo's best interests. Ward's excommunication was halted and a pe-

Dispensation of Thomas F. Ward from the Order of St. Benedict. (St. Leo Archives.)

tition to release him from the Benedictine Order was placed before the Mother Abbey in Rome, St. Anselm of the City. On January 23, 1897, his dispensation was sent out from the Holy See by Innocent Wolf, O.S.B., president of the American-Cassinensis Congregation. It reads, in translation from the Latin:

> We note and attest that Frater Placidus (Thomas F.) Ward in the Priory of St. Leo, professed in simple vows, has left the Community and State of Florida freely and willingly, and the Reverend Prior Charles petitions from us the dismissal of the aforementioned Brother Placidus. Having considered the reasons given to us and having listened to the counsel of the visitators we hereby dismiss the aforementioned Frater Placidus (Thomas F. Ward) from our Congregation, so that he is free from every bond and obligation of simple vows.[6]

No documents have survived in Rome that might show Father Charles's second thoughts about Placidus Ward.[7] His "reasons given to us"—in the

words of Rome's edict—remain veiled. Ward's contrition and the moral authority of a Jesuit priest may have been sufficient grounds for Mohr to yield. Also, as the minutes of their hasty meeting of October 21, 1896, show, the monks had initially agreed to Placidus's release, and the prior's continuing refusal to concur could eventually have caused them embarrassment. Perhaps by now Father Charles was simply tired of the affair. The daily management of a busy priory—soon to become an abbey—needed his full attention, not the discontent of a former monk eight hundred miles away.

The document of dispensation offers another clue about what may have happened. The German-born Abbot Innocent Wolf (1843–1922), the signatory of Ward's formal release, was one of his generation's most esteemed Benedictines, the first abbot (1876–1921) of St. Benedict's Abbey in Atchison, Kansas. A well-traveled but frail priest, he was in Rome that winter "trying to recover his health."[8] Abbot Wolf was a humble, scholarly priest who abided criticism within his religious community so long as it was given openly. But he was contemptuous and censorious of the common practice of "murmuring," as the Benedictines called a monk's secret criticism of his superiors. Perhaps Father de Carriere knew that Father Charles would have to address Ward's case to Innocent Wolf and, consequently, emphasized repeatedly that Ward had never said *anything* bad about anyone at St. Leo. Unfortunately, Innocent Wolf's extensive diaries (in German), in the St. Benedict Abbey archives, contain no mention of Thomas F. Ward.[9]

A plausible scenario for the resolution of Ward's crisis can be constructed. In the late 1800s Roman Catholic canon law required that a monk leaving a monastic order must receive his dispensation in person, either from the bishop of the diocese where he lived or from a delegated authority.[10] To comply with this demand, Ward must have traveled from Shreveport to Nachitoches, Louisiana (seventy-five miles south by riverboat), where the Diocese was then centered at the Cathedral of the Immaculate Conception. In this remote location, Thomas F. Ward's long struggle with the Order of St. Benedictine would have finally ended.[11]

✦ In Shreveport in August 1988, I discovered nothing more about Ward than the newspapers' notices of his arrival on that frigid January day in 1897. Completed in 1896, the old Holy Trinity Church, which he must have visited, still stood, but its registers gave no evidence of his presence. A parking lot occupies the site where the City Hotel had been, and a plaque indicates

where the nearby Grand Opera House (1,200 seats) had been located, and where, the *Shreveport Times* of January 8 noted, Sidney R. Ellis's *Darkest Russia*— "the most intense and realistic play seen in years . . . depicting Russia as it is today . . . replete with effects, groupings and tableaux"—was playing when Ward arrived.

In a now familiar pattern, Thomas Ward's name failed to surface in either Shreveport's municipal records or any documents of Caddo Parish, Louisiana, dating to the turn of the century. Again, he seemed to have vanished. Any new clues would have to be discovered in that last letter from "P.O. Box 54," an address that left no trail in the bureaucracy of the U.S. Post Office. *He had stable employment.* ("I propose, commencing this month to send [Father Charles] ten dollars every month," he had written to de Carriere.) Searching through microfilms, I found the following report in the *Shreveport Herald* of January 11, 1897: "Incidentally it may be mentioned that the Holy Trinity Academy today has reopened after a vacation of two weeks. There are three professors engaged in teaching the youth of this institution."

I wondered whether this announcement, published less than a week after Ward's arrival in Shreveport, might have referred indirectly to him. Distantly removed from Father Charles's censure, he could again have found employment within the Catholic Church. According to the Shreveport directory of 1897, the Holy Trinity Academy (at 314 Marshall Street) employed Rev. S. B. Scharl as director and Professor J. P. Mueller as principal. As described in a separate advertisement, it was a "Select Day School for Boys" with a course of studies both classical and commercial, commencing annually at the beginning of September and closing in the "latter part of June." Perhaps Ward, hired for the second semester just starting in January 1897, was the third professor mentioned in the newspaper ad. A departure from Shreveport after the school year might be suggested by the name "T. C. Ward" [sic] found among the listings for "Unclaimed Letters," printed ten months later in the *Shreveport Times* of October 24. These conjectures cannot be confirmed, however, for none of the Holy Trinity Academy's records have survived.

Even if he did teach at the academy, where did he then go? Perhaps he lay among nameless dead in Shreveport's old Catholic cemetery. The voluminous sexton's reports in the municipal archives soon disproved this theory. The possibilities for Ward's whereabouts now seemed infinite. A drive thirty-five miles west to Marshall, Texas, brought no results, but Inez Hughes, the historian of Harrison County—and the high school teacher of Bill Moyers—

listened with curiosity to my story while searching through town and church documents and chatting about the old town's history. A nonproductive exchange of letters with the historical society of Hot Springs, Arkansas, an easy destination for a consumptive in this part of the South, made the prospect of any new development seem especially bleak. Thomas F. Ward had once again eluded my search.

→ Back in New York, I began writing to municipal historical societies and state departments of vital statistics north and west of Louisiana. Then, out of the blue, from the Texas History Collection of the Dallas Public Library, Joan L. Dobson responded on October 17, 1988, to my routine inquiry. It was the letter I had long hoped for. Her first sentence was electrifying: "Well, I did not find your Thomas F. Ward in the Dallas City directories, but something made me look a little further."

"Something" had indeed compelled her to search beyond my request in one of the few old Houston city directories in her collection, and in the 1905 directory of Dallas's rival city she found the name Thomas F. Ward, a "music teacher" living at a boardinghouse at 218 Crawford Street. He had settled in the town most likely to be avoided by a consumptive: the hot and humid port of Houston, Texas. It was the most unexpected of outcomes. The end of the search now seemed in sight!

An immediate telephone investigation into the city directories of the Houston Public Library produced a portrait of a restless man struggling to put down roots in this bustling southern city. Ward's new home was a frontier town yearning to become a metropolis, a constantly changing place that— unlike Dallas and San Antonio—had not found its own identity and that— like its new inhabitant—was restlessly on the move. Houstonians were preoccupied with their city's imminent greatness and with its new wealth (reflected in the oil wells being capped daily nearby). A snobbish upper class took pride in the city's growing cultural awareness.

Ward probably arrived in 1898, for his name first surfaces in the 1899 city directory as a boarder at 1311 Dallas Avenue, in what today is the sky-scraper-dominated downtown area. At the end of the nineteenth century, however, that first home was located near the center of a manufacturing, railroad, and educational area rapidly approaching 45,000 inhabitants. Over the next decade he moved to at least five other lodgings within that district,

Corner of Main Street and Texas Avenue, Houston, Texas, 1904. (Houston Public Library.)

all within a short walking distance from the city's oldest Catholic Church, the Annunciation Church (founded 1869). The following addresses suggest Ward's search for stability in a culturally unfamiliar locale: rooms in 1900–1901 at 1206 Travis Street (now in the heart of high-tech Houston's architectural eruption); a boarding house in 1902–3 at 1308 Lamar Avenue (a luxurious modern hotel today); a lodging the following year, 1903–4, at 218 Crawford Street (now a parking lot); four years later, in 1907, rooms at 1812 Polk Avenue (in the path of a super highway today); and finally, in 1908–9, a boardinghouse at 1508 Congress Avenue, his last known address (now also one of the ubiquitous parking lots that compete for space with the city's skyscrapers). Three years later his name disappears after the 1911–12 directory, where he is incorrectly listed as "Ward, Thomas R., musician."

Certain things could now be guessed. Thomas F. Ward, a devout Catholic to the end, must have died in 1912 and been buried in a Catholic cemetery near the downtown area. A phone call to the Catholic Cemetery Office in Houston immediately confirmed these suspicions. Officials there soon searched out and forwarded to me cemetery records that pointed unmistakably to a pathetic ending to his life.

Burial records of Thomas F. Ward in Holy Cross Cemetery. Interment card and cemetery ledger. (Office of Catholic Cemeteries, Houston.)

The final document about Thomas F. Ward's life, the interment record, also distorts his name. It states that "F. T. Ward" died on May 15, 1912, and was buried the following day at the Holy Cross Cemetery in grave number 407 in section P of the graveyard, an area known as "Strangers' Rest." I soon discovered that "Strangers' Rest" was a euphemism for a section set aside for those who died alone or whose families were too destitute to pay for burial. His companions on the roster for section P were principally Mexicans, as well as some immigrant Italians and Irish. The accounts of Holy Cross Cemetery indicated that the ten dollar burial fee for "F. T. Ward" was paid in cash—half by "Professor Diehl" and half from "charity" contributed by "Father Hennessy" of the Catholic Church. There was no stone for Ward's plot, but Pat DeLucia of the Catholic Cemetery Office informed me by phone on

October 24, 1988, that the marker could easily be dug up to verify the location.

The obituaries in Houston's two principal papers, quickly searched out, verified that Ward's long battle with chronic sickness had finally ended in spring 1912. The *Houston Chronicle* obituary on May 17, 1912, read: "Ward— At a private sanitarium in Houston, May 15, T. F. Ward, a musician, Funeral Thursday at 5 p.m. from the parlors of Settegast & Kopf, with interment in Holy Cross Cemetery. Rev. Father Hennessy officiated." The *Houston Post* obituary on the same day added an interesting detail: "The funeral of T. F. Ward was held yesterday afternoon at 5 o'clock under the auspices of the local Musicians union." On May 19, the *Houston Post* listed him among forty-two residents who had died that week and stated the cause of death—the outcome I had feared but expected: "T. F. Ward, male, white, 57 years; pulmonary tuberculosis."

Erasing all doubt about the identity of the resident of 1508 Congress Street, the U.S. Census of 1910 now confirmed that Thomas F. Ward, aged "53" in 1910, born in the State of New York of parents both from Ireland, had been as recently as April of 1910 gainfully employed as a "musician" for more than a year. It showed also that he considered his profession as "Orchestra"—in other words, an orchestra musician.[12]

But these few facts seemed only to deepen the mystery surrounding Ward's obscure death in Houston, after years of employment as a "musician" and "music teacher." How could circumstances have brought him to poverty and burial in an unmarked grave only two years later? One by one the new clues led to an impasse. Of eleven sanitariums listed in the 1912 city directory, none exist today. The records of the Catholic sanitarium, St. Joseph's Infirmary (now St. Joseph's Hospital), were lost in a fire many years after Ward's death. The funeral home Settegast & Kopf, still in business in 1988, had long since thrown away its oldest records. No official death certificate for Ward was on file with the Texas State Bureau of Vital Statistics in Austin,[13] even though by 1912 the state required registration. Presumably a "private sanitarium" would have observed the law and submitted the required information. Why did it not? But most disappointing, the Annunciation Church's own death records of its parishioners, carefully recorded since 1871, are missing for May 1912, and no one at the Church today can explain what happened to them.[14] Instead of establishing a satisfactory account of Ward's last months, I had to accede to the scant facts of the two newspaper obituaries, which now raised as many questions as they answered.

When Thomas Ward (Paul/Peter/Placidus) confronted Benedict Roth in 1894 he had been hale and hearty on returning from North Carolina—a fact worthy of Father Benedict's diary. In the eighteen intervening years he had experienced physical ordeals of flight, anxiety, joblessness, and travel. Moving his possessions repeatedly, he had lived for fourteen years in one of the most uncomfortable environments in the country. He had fought his disease tenaciously for decades before finally surrendering in a Houston sanitarium. How had he arrived there?

→ In November 1988, I traveled to Houston hoping to find answers to these questions. A strange time warp seemed to usher in the last stage of my search. On locating Ward's first address at 1311 Dallas Avenue, I found myself staring up at the gleaming Four Seasons Hotel and, studying my city maps in the hotel lounge, I overheard Texas oil men in ten-gallon hats discussing huge money deals. His next address, at 1812 Polk Avenue, brought me to the Eastex Expressway, where frenzied rush-hour traffic overhead made me wish that most of a century had not gone by. My visit to the local Musicians Union brought bemused but friendly smiles at such an eccentric misuse of one's time. "Why on earth would we keep records about a union member who died seventy-five years ago?" an official asked. "Would you like to hear the orchestra rehearsing next door for Frank Sinatra's and Sammy Davis Jr.'s concert?" The imposing neo-Gothic Church of the Annunciation, however, was still standing at the juncture of Crawford and Texas Streets, little changed since Ward's time. At least some things remain the same—even in Houston.

The Church of the Annunciation seemed now to offer a solution. Perhaps something about Thomas Ward could be discovered in the careers of the two men who had paid for and attended his funeral in the Church's cemetery: Professor Diehl and Father Hennessy. Their concern and generosity suggested that they were his good friends. In the next years, reading through microfilm of the *Houston Post* and *Chronicle*, it might be possible to reconstruct Ward's long stay in Houston. In searching for the names of Diehl and Hennessy, I had only to keep my attention focused on religion and music, and—surely—Thomas F. Ward would again emerge.

→ Anton Diehl (1867–1952), a native of Wiesbaden, Germany, arrived in Houston in 1884 at age seventeen and by 1900 had become widely known as an orchestra leader, violin teacher, and founder of Houston's best-known

Sketch of the Church
of the Annunciation,
Houston, 1871.
(Courtesy Annuncia-
tion Church.)

music school—the Anton Diehl Conservatory.[15] Diehl was always described
as a first-rate violinist. The *Chronicle* of April 13, 1903, reported that he made
his Houston conducting debut on April 1, 1892, with Johann Nepomuk
Hummel's *Mass in D*, thereby beginning a fifty-year-long association with music
at the Church of the Annunciation. On June 7, 1903, the *Post* observed that
he had been "the leading violinist of our city for many years now and he
isn't an old man either."

The Anton Diehl Conservatory was a "Select School of Music" according
to frequent advertisements in local society papers; in its heyday (1905–8) it
was reputed to be the most complete school of its kind in the South.[16] A
founding member of the local branch of the American Federation of Musicians (1897) and of the Houston Symphony Orchestra (1913), Diehl accomplished "perhaps as much as any other man for the development of interest in music in Houston and South Texas [and was] a man of splendid

Anton Diehl and his Conservatory of Music, ca. 1907. (Courtesy of Leland A. Dolan.)

cultural attainments."[17] It was inevitable that Diehl, a devout Catholic and a musician, would eventually meet Thomas F. Ward.

In his first years in Houston, Ward seems not to have performed publicly but instead to have made his living by giving piano, organ, and composition lessons to private students in Houston and at St. Mary's Seminary in La Porte, on Galveston Bay a short train ride away. One of Ward's students in La Porte, James L. Drummond, later became organist of Houston's Sacred Heart Catholic Church.[18] Since the seminary's few surviving records (covering the period from 1906 to 1912) reveal nothing of Ward's presence, we can safely assume that he had resigned from the school by 1906.[19] The names of any other of his pupils, after ninety years, cannot be brought to light.[20]

Recurring tuberculosis probably caused Ward to remain inactive in a city offering many opportunities for public performance. Even the Annunciation Church's benefit concert on May 16, 1901, for victims of the Great Jacksonville Fire—the fire that destroyed Ward's former church—failed to draw him out, though Houston's leading musicians all were to take part, as the *Post* announced on May 12. Surely, if he had been well, he would have performed on this occasion.

Ward's experiences in Jacksonville's social orchestras, however, made him well-qualified to perform inconspicuously with similar groups in Houston

and to supplement what must have been a meager income. In the late spring of 1903 he suddenly surfaced—for the first time—named by the *Post* on June 7 as a violist in the twelve-man orchestra scheduled to play for Anton Diehl's wedding to Gabrielle Marie Lavielle on June 10, 1903. Ward's ability to play viola—previously unsuspected—is thus mentioned for the first and only time. The principal celebrant at the Church of the Annunciation was Rev. Thomas Hennessy. The attendance at the gala wedding was "probably the largest in the history of Houston," stated the *Post* in its "Society" column of June 14; the ceremonies, decorations, and music were elaborately described by both newspapers. On June 13 the *Chronicle* mused that "the special program of music rendered before the ceremony was most beautiful." And on June 14 the *Post* noted that Edmund Kretschmer's "Coronation March," played by the full orchestra with organ, was "grand and glorious." Wagner's "Bridal Chorus" (from *Lohengrin*), the paper added, was accompanied by a fifteen-member women's chorus with orchestral accompaniment. Later, "the tender strains and pure harmonies of Schumann's 'Voices of Love' fell gently on the ear."

According to the Houston city directory of 1904, Ward considered himself to be a "musician" rather than a "music teacher," and therefore we can safely assume that he was a member of Diehl's society orchestra. "Diehl's Orchestra," as it was known in Houston, performed at weddings, debutante balls, holiday dances, and private parties held in the city's mansions and in restaurants and hotels where the latest fashions and one's social status could be paraded. Typical of such occasions was the ball staged in the Concordia Club's hall in 1905 by Mrs. Therese Lorenzen, who, the *Houstonian* of November 18 recounted, "entertained with a handsome cotillion in honor of her daughter. . . . The chandeliers were entwined with Japanese fern. . . . The stage, quite hidden with tall palms, was occupied by Diehl's orchestra, which rendered inspiring and beautiful music for the merry dancers. . . . Eight numbers and three cotillions were danced, the figures of the latter being among the most novel and effective of the season." (For larger private gatherings and public concerts, Diehl's orchestra often joined that of violinist Ben Schram to become Diehl and Schram's Orchestra or, in a spirit of compromise, Schram and Diehl's Orchestra.)

We can also predict the kind of entertainment music Ward performed outside Diehl's orchestra, either on piano, organ, violin, or viola. In the early 1900s, a typical musical ensemble in Houston's fancier dining establishments consisted of a piano trio or quartet (sometimes with a wind instrument

added), which performed lighter classical selections from Schubert to Lehár. The group also performed an occasional ragtime or a sentimental popular medley for the "cotillions." The music created a genial, almost Viennese ambience for the dignified clientele of locales such as the popular Sauter's Restaurant.[21]

As 1903 ended, Ward also became visible in Houston's serious concert life. At a November 20 benefit concert—part of a bazaar sponsored by the Young Ladies' Circle of the Shearn Methodist Church—he performed Tchaikovsky's "Barcarole" ("June" from the *Seasons,* op. 37a) and Maurice Moszkowski's "Momento giojoso" (from the *Trois Morceaux Poétiques,* op. 42), the one's pensive lyricism followed by the other's picturesque virtuosity. Though both newspapers announced that "Mr. Thomas Ward" would be the pianist, the *Post* later reported on November 22 that "Mrs. Thomas F. Ward"(!) had performed on a concert "far above the average both in the character of the selections and the style of execution." Presumably the reviewer failed to attend the concert he described, a custom still occasionally followed today. Perhaps the paper's "Mrs." was simply a typographical error.

No catalogues of the Diehl Conservatory have survived to verify Ward's presence on its faculty. However, press coverage of its artists' recitals over several years and Diehl's own newspaper advertisements suggest strongly that Ward was never at the school. Diehl's prominent ad in the *Post* of August 18, 1907, for example, listing the school's fifteen-member faculty in detail, does not mention Ward. In 1906 the Conservatory acquired a large pipe organ and a sizable library of music scores and books—necessitating the establishment of the "Diehl Musical Library Association," fulsomely described in the *Houston Post* on September 2 and 11. For its main concert that fall, the faculty offered a recital of Liszt, Haydn, MacDowell, and Gounod, together with "the weird music of Grieg, the Norwegian wizard . . . selections worthy of any artists and any audience," as the *Post* flamboyantly observed on November 18. Again, Ward's name is not mentioned.

Diehl's pipe organ instructor was G. W. Heinzelman, a noted local church organist, and his principal piano teacher was Mary Elizabeth Rouse, a skilled interpreter who, ironically, had studied in Leipzig with Delius's harmony teacher, Carl Reinecke (1824–1910). The *Post* reported on February 24, 1907, that Rouse had performed Reinecke's "Ballade" for piano at the conservatory the previous week. In all likelihood Ward's tuberculosis prevented him from working daily at Houston's most stimulating cultural institution—to the loss of the city's musical life.

III.
Momento giojoso.

Maurice Moszkowski,
Oeuvre 42 Nº III.

Edition Peters.   7120

Maurice Moszkowski, "Momento giojoso," from Trois Morceaux Poétiques, op. 42 (1887). (Archives of C. F. Peters Corporation, New York.)

Also performing at the Young Ladies' Circle bazaar in 1907, alongside the inexplicable "Mrs. Thomas F. Ward," was the violinist Gustav Edward Von Hofe, "a recent accession to the ranks of Houston's musicians," according to the Post of November 15. Von Hofe dazzled his audience with a "Serenade" by the now forgotten Polish composer Roman Statkowski (1860–1925) and a "Bolero" by the once popular German composer Carl Bohm (1844–1920), the latter piece "in response to an enthusiastic encore demand," the paper noted on November 22. Despite dissimilar musical tastes—Ward's Tchaikovsky/Moszkowski was patently superior to Von Hofe's Statkowski/Bohm—Von Hofe and Ward were to work together closely during the year ahead.

At the time of Ward's November debut, all of musical Houston was looking forward to an event of special significance: the local premiere of Alfred
Gaul's cantata, *The Holy City*, scheduled for performance in the Houston Opera
House (Turner Hall) in early 1904. Von Hofe had been named director of
soloists, orchestra, and chorus, and Ward had been appointed rehearsal pianist. The production, featuring the popular "Cecilian Octette," would bring
together many of the city's religious and secular musical organizations. Covering rehearsals at Grunewald's Music Store on Main Street, the *Post* reported
on December 6, 1903, that the singers were given "a thorough drill . . . [in
which] Mr. Ward played throughout an unassertive but sustaining accompaniment." Each week brought new press commentary about the importance
of the forthcoming event.

The *Holy City* (1882), by the English composer Alfred Robert Gaul (1837–
1913), may seem tepid stuff today, a pious imitation of Mendelssohn even,
but in Victorian England (and in America) the "superficial fluency" of Gaul's
many cantatas, psalm-settings, anthems, and hymns made his music widely
popular.[22]

Gaul described his cantata as "almost entirely reflective" and reassured
performers that "with the exception of two hymns, a verse from Milton, and
three verses from the Te Deum, the words are entirely scriptural."[23] Attending a full rehearsal, the *Post*'s critic of January 10, 1904, heard in the cantata
"musical force and charming climaxes, fugues and double choruses," as well
as "dash, energy, and effects that combine beauty and elegance upon such a
noble subject."

Perhaps Thomas Ward understood Gaul's advocation of the contemplative
life and his admonition to renounce the material world in anticipation of
forever dwelling in the New Jerusalem—the Holy City. But someone—perhaps Von Hofe—sensed that a glittering audience, many of whose members
enjoyed the leisure made possible by the city's oil "gushers," needed a more
cheerful send-off than Gaul's stern tenor aria: "For like as a father pitieth his
children even so is the Lord merciful to them that fear Him." To correct this
shortcoming, Dudley Buck's anthem "There Is a River" was inserted into the
cantata, and the work was given a new ending featuring the Cecilian Octette:
Frederick Stevenson's *May Day (Rustic Dance)*, a setting for chorus of an Elizabe-
than ballad, which the *Post* promised would be "entirely different in construction from the program numbers . . . a light and cheerful climax to the
evening's pleasure. This is a number brimming with the spirit of rustic mer-

Turner Hall

TUESDAY, JANUARY 12

"The HOLY CITY"

A Sacred Cantata

By Alfred R. Gaul.

Suggested by the passages of Scripture, elevating and inspiring.

With the exception of two hymns, a verse from Milton and three verses from the Te Deum, the Words are entirely Scriptural.

The Fuges and unaccompanied choruses and trios, as well as the double choruses and every number of the work will be taken in its entirety. Soloists, Mrs. N. C. Munger, Misses Camille Bradburn and Bessie Hughes, Messrs. Fred Juenger, Gould, Harry Griswald and George Meyer, assisted by a well trained choir of select voices and the Cecilian Octette society.

Two extra numbers will have their first presentation South and tend to show the versatility of the choir. The orchestra is composed of the best the profession affords, including Messrs. Anton Diehl and Ben Schram, Mr. G. E. Von Hofe. director; Messrs. Aldridge, Kidd and Thomas F. Ward accompanists.

Price of Admission 50c.

Turner Hall, Tuesday, January 12th, 8:00 p. m.

Advertisement for Alfred R. Gaul's *The Holy City*. (*Houston Post*, January 10, 1904.)

riment; its accompaniment is a four-hand piano score which Messrs. Thomas F. Ward and Aldridge Kidd will play" (January 10, 1904). The advertisement for the concert appeared in the Sunday *Post* of January 10, 1904. Completely forgotten now, Frederick Stevenson (1845–1925) was an English Catholic organist and composer of sacred choral music (a pupil of Sir George Macfarren). He moved to Denver, Colorado, in 1883 and after 1894 was active in Los Angeles and Santa Barbara. His *May Day* for chorus and orchestra was written in 1895.

On the day after the January 12, 1904, performance (admission "50 cents"), the newspapers' music critics competed with each other in expressions of cultural boosterism. The *Post* considered the concert of "high grade music . . . brilliant [and] throughout so artistically presented as not only to delight the audience, but in a way educate those who heard and cause the hearts of loyal Houstonians to beat with pride in the performances of our home people." The *Chronicle* pronounced it a "splendid success [by] home talent that any city could well be proud to claim." The concluding *May Day*, it added, "made the rafters ring with the concerted music of the beautifully blending voices of the entire number. . . . Mr. Aldridge Kidd, accompanist, was assisted in the last number by Thomas Ward."

Frederick Stevenson, *May Day* (1895). Two-piano introduction. (Library of Congress.)

Ward's demotion to Aldridge Kidd's "assistant" in the piano duo accompaniment can be explained. The Kidd family was perhaps the most prominent musical family in Houston during Ward's time. Mrs. Kate B. (George) Kidd was a noted patron of the arts. Her son, the estimable pianist Aldridge Kidd, gave frequent recitals in Houston; her daughter Mary Carson Kidd had studied and sung in Italy and was a popular local artist.

The *Post* returned to the subject of the concert several days later, expressing its opinion on January 17 that Gaul's cantata "rank[ed] well with the more largely ambitious oratorios of old composers" and that the orchestral

accompaniments "satisfied the cultivated artistic sense." Singling out Von Hofe's conducting, it added, "the singing of that old Seventeenth Century rustic dance song, 'May Day,' made a charming finale to an evening of pure musical pleasure, and the style in which it was given as a mixed chorus has never been surpassed in Houston." It should be noted that, as violin soloist, Anton Diehl, whose orchestra provided the nucleus of the eighteen-piece accompaniment, shared in the glory.

Three weeks after the concert, in celebration of his great success, Von Hofe—by now known locally as Ed—held a "Reception-Musicale" (by invitation only) at the Masonic Hall, with dance music provided courtesy of Schram and Diehl's Orchestra. In all likelihood, Ward, as a member of the Diehl ensemble, performed once more as an "accompanist"—in the salon compositions of Friedrich von Flotow, Otto Hackh, and Saverio Mercadante cited in the Post on February 11. More than fifty couples attended the "thoroughly delightful affair" at which the orchestra "discoursed sweet sounds" and where "a delicious brew of punch was served all during the evening and everybody had the best kind of a time," the Post effused on February 14. Although Von Hofe made plans to repeat his success with The Holy City "on a more appropriate scale, with an augmented chorus of sixty voices," and even held rehearsals, the Post noted on May 4, his project seems never to have materialized. But long afterward, the public's memory of The Holy City had not disappeared and periodically over the next decade excerpts from the popular cantata were performed in Houston's churches and public concerts.

The Holy City established Ed Von Hofe's local reputation and quickly furthered his career. Three months later, just before the Easter services of 1904, he was named organist of the Annunciation Church, under Anton Diehl's directorship, the Post reported on March 27. His photograph appeared in the newspaper on April 22 as one of Houston's seven most prominent musical directors—the director of the city's esteemed Cecilian Octette. Later in the fall, the Church completely overhauled its organ in time for its newly famous organist and choir master to perform music by American composers—an organ work by Dudley Buck and a mass by Harrison Millard, all dutifully noted in the Post on October 9. Ward, a member of its congregation, must have noted Von Hofe's rapid advancement in Catholic musical circles.

The Holy City was only one example of the "high grade music" Thomas Ward must have experienced in Houston. As the twentieth century began, music gradually assumed an important role in the city's cultural life. The two

principal newspapers reviewed local and visiting artists as well as church concerts—the *Post* in its Sunday "Tête-à-Tête with the Musicians" and the *Chronicle* (after 1901) in its weekly "Music and Musicians" column, written by Mrs. Wille Hutcheson and Sam T. Swinford, respectively. Lenient in their assessments of native talent, Houston's two critics covered concerts by the Treble Clef Club, the Cecilian Octette, the Houston Quartette Society, the [choral] Festival Association, the Women's Choral Club, and the Symphony Club, as well as countless solo recitals by hometown artists. Local music programs included a curious mixture of classic and romantic masters (Haydn, Chopin, Liszt, and others), "contemporary music" (Debussy, MacDowell, Ethelbert Nevin, Gabriel Fauré), sentimental salon music ("Footsteps in the Snow," "By the Sycamore Tree," etc.), and "patriotic airs" ("Dixie," "The Yellow Rose of Texas"). A plethora of Wards can be found among Houston's performers, always confusing the search for the real Thomas F. Ward! Among other forgotten Wards were W. D. Ward, violinist at the Annunciation Church in 1901; Mrs. E. C. Ward, a noted local soprano and performer in the Protestant churches; C. E. and J. H. Ward, organists at Shearn Methodist Church; and Annie Bird Ward, a Houston pianist of strong musicianship who presented superior classical repertory and always elicited good reviews. Not satisfied by live concerts, the music-thirsty public (after 1911) began attending "Victrola Recitals" at Goggan's Music Store on Main Street—a premonition perhaps of Houston's future fascination with high technology.

Among the international artists performing in Houston during Ward's time were Ernestine Schumann-Heink (1903), Adelina Patti (1904), Vladimir de Pachmann (1904, 1912), Nellie Melba (1905), Rudolph Ganz (1907), Josef Hofmann (1911), and Maud Powell (1911)—to cite only a few of the more famous. The Chicago Symphony Orchestra (conducted by Adolf Rosenbecker), the Pittsburgh Symphony (Emil Paur), the New York Symphony Orchestra (Walter Damrosch), and the Russian Symphony (Modest Altschuler) all made their way to Houston, as did the New York Metropolitan Opera's touring company. The Russian Symphony's concerts of April 1911, featuring works of Tchaikovsky, Dvořák, Grieg, and Wagner, were described by Sam Swinford as "the greatest feast of music they have ever had in this city." Swinford believed that the time was now at hand for Houston to have its own symphony orchestra: "The orchestra will come sooner or later. . . . Judging by the past there is every reason to expect only the brightest future for musical Houston."[24]

Swinford's prophecy was fulfilled the year after Ward's death, when the Houston Symphony Orchestra presented its first concert on December 19, 1913, described at length in the *Post* on December 19 and 20. Among the violinists for that program, conducted by Julien Paul Blitz and featuring Haydn's *London Symphony*, was Anton Diehl.

❖ The second person attending Thomas Ward's funeral was even more widely known than Anton Diehl: Father Thomas Hennessy (1836–1913), the pastor of Houston's Annunciation Church and the city's leading Catholic. Rev. Hennessy's church, a Houston landmark, had witnessed the city's development "from a straggling prairie village into the foremost city of Texas," as the *Chronicle* of October 15, 1911, respectfully observed.

Born in Tipperary, Ireland, in 1836, Father Hennessy had spent much of his youth in the frontier settlements of the western United States. On June 22, 1913, the *Post* described his Texas past: "On mule-back or afoot, through the sweltering heat of the sun-baked plains, or the raging blizzards of the storm-swept prairie, climbing hazardous passages, fording swollen rivers, threading a way through the trackless piney woods, Father Hennessy sought the members of his flock and ministered to them."

Since coming to the Annunciation Church in 1879, his concern for the poor had endeared him to Houstonians, among whom it was said "the ragged newsboy on the corner knew his genial soul as well as the moneyed people of the office buildings, and all loved him," the *Chronicle* proclaimed on November 21, 1913, the day of the beloved churchman's death. We can understand why Ward would have admired and befriended Hennessy. A decade before, around the time Ward might have become acquainted with him, the Catholics claimed that, according to the *Post* of November 22, 1903, "conservatively . . . more than 1,000 members of the papal Church in Houston" attended the city's five Catholic churches. Father Hennessy was the undisputed leader of this flock. The priest "was a learned man, who thought mere learning accomplished little" and—with the same unshakable faith of his parishioner Ward—possessed "a touch of violence, especially in defense of the Church." When Father Hennessy died, the *Houston Chronicle*'s front-page headline described his funeral as the largest in Houston's history, attended by thousands of mourners.

As Ward's confessor, Hennessy must have been aware of his friend's unhappy years at St. Leo, his banishment from Florida, and—perhaps—the rea-

CHRONICLE

NOVEMBER 19, 1913   TWENTY

Father Hennessy Dead

❂ ❂ ❂ ❂ ❂ ❂ ❂

Loved Dean of Houston Clergy Is Gone

▓▓▓▓▓ FATHER THOMAS HENNESSY ▓▓▓▓▓

Found Sleeping in Death in His Chair After Performing
the Duties of His Calling; Had Just Dined.

DEATH, sudden, silent and painless, invaded the parish house
of the Church of the Annunciation at 1 o'clock Wednesday
afternoon, stretched its hands over Rev. Father Thomas Hennessy and claimed him as its own.

Father Thomas F. Hennessy. (*Houston Chronicle,*
November 19, 1913.)

sons behind his abandonment of the Benedictine Order. Did he also know about Ward's superior musical gifts? The answer to this question lay buried in the pages of the *Houston Post* of January 17, 1904: On January 11, in celebration of Father Hennessy's twenty-five years at the church, Thomas Ward, piano, and Anton Diehl, violin, accompanied the Annunciation choir in a special hymn opening the ceremonies and, at the reception later (in company with Odin Kendall), rendered "two very pretty [unnamed] trios."

By this time Ward seems already to have established a reputation as a "fast study," a musician who could be called upon in an emergency. In 1903 the Annunciation Church's organist was Cheston Heath, a Harvard graduate who had studied music at the Boston Conservatory. For the 1903 Christmas service (three weeks before Father Hennessy's ceremony/reception), the organist had prepared an ambitious program in collaboration with Anton Diehl and his orchestra. On December 27 the *Post* described how Heath had been suddenly called to the nearby protestant Christ Church "at almost the last moment to take charge of Christmas day music": "[Heath] got Mr. Ward to

take his place for the 10 o'clock high mass. [Paolo] Giorza's Mass No. 1 was grandly sung at the Church of the Annunciation. Each and every one of the nine soloists rendered this beautiful devotional music most fittingly. The Diehl orchestral accompaniments greatly enriched the service."

His musical professionalism must have made a powerful impression on Rev. Hennessy, for at the end of 1903, after a seventeen-year hiatus, Thomas F. Ward once again was appointed organist and music director of a Catholic church. It must have been spiritually fulfilling for him to return to the role he had known best—to the source of his musical identity. He served the Annunciation Church in a contingency capacity until March 1904, when he turned over the post to Von Hofe, the musical hero of *The Holy City*.

Later that year another emergency arose when, for reasons unknown, Von Hofe suddenly left Houston just before the 1904 Christmas service, and Ward was again called upon to save the situation at the Annunciation Church. The *Post* reported on New Year's Day 1905 that "the grand music sung in the Church of the Annunciation on Christmas Day will be repeated at the service of today. . . . Mr. Ward is organist." The mass performed would be Bonifazio Asioli's "number 3 (the biggest one)," the paper added. Without naming him, the *Post* of that Christmas Day reveals that the organist (i.e., Ward) opened the service with Bach's *Fantasia and Fugue in A Minor* (BWV.561) and closed it with the *Fugue in G Minor* (BWV.578). The Bach performances that had so impressed Fritz Delius two decades earlier once more found an appreciative audience.

Just before Easter of 1905, Ward *again* inexplicably relinquished his church position—this time to Mrs. George Bruce, who was to serve as the Annunciation's organist for most of the next decade. After New Year's Day 1905, Thomas F. Ward's name never again appears in Houston's newspapers until the announcement of his death more than seven years later. The *Chronicle* of March 12, 1911, lists more than seven hundred names of Houston's musicians and patrons of music, but Ward's is not among them. A recently discovered newspaper clipping from the *Post* of February 8, 1914, confirms that he preceded Von Hofe and Bruce as "director and organist" at the Annunciation and summarizes his brief tenure: "Prof. Ward, who died the early part of last year . . . was a thorough musician and made a splendid director. He had a large library."[25] A measure of Ward's total obscurity by this time lies in the fact that he had died not "the early part of last year" but almost two years before this article was published.

I have discovered nothing concrete that would explain Ward's mysterious retreat from the Annunciation Church in 1905 or his absence thereafter from the music programs of any other Catholic Churches in the Houston-Galveston area. Alone with his music and library during his remaining years, he seems to have withdrawn into a tranquil spiritual life, to have become "lost to the world"—in the words of Gustav Mahler's famous song of spiritual resignation. In this circumstance, did Ward sometimes reflect on Florida and his gifted, spirited student of a generation ago?

I eventually found the answer to this question. In a most improbable turn of events, Delius's own name suddenly appeared in the newspaper from which Ward's had disappeared: the *Houston Post*. On December 15, 1907, the paper published a clipping "from the *London Times*" brought to its attention by "a scholarly musician, a resident of Houston." It was a commentary on Delius's *Appalachia*, which had received its English premiere on November 22, only three weeks earlier, by the London New Symphony Orchestra under the direction of the German conductor Fritz Cassirer. The commentary's surprising contents follow:

Englishman's "Appalachia"

It really seems as though the Yorkshire composer, Mr. Frederick Delius, is about to be recognized by his countrymen. His pianoforte concerto was played at one of the recent Queen's Hall promenade concerts and on Friday evening [November 22, 1907] was produced at the same hall [as] his orchestral variations, entitled "Appalachia," which, it may be well to mention, is the aboriginal name for America. *The variations are built on an old negro song which Mr. Delius heard nightly when he was an orange grower in Florida.* The melody is remarkable for all the notes, with the exception of three unimportant ones, being contained in the common chord, that of C major. This renders the tune really distinguishable, but it might also have tended to monotony had it not been for the genius of the composer. His design was to express his impressions of the vast forests on the banks of the [river], the sounds in the stillness of night and the brilliancy of day, and he has succeeded in producing a work of remarkable emotional power, ranging in sentiment from grave to gay, and touching on the mysterious. There are fourteen variations, into some of which are introduced phrases of the slave song, but merely vocalized to "La." At the thirteenth variation the full chorus deliver[s] the song allied to words descriptive of the dawn. The finale opens

with a short baritone solo, followed by a male voice chorus and the subsequent entry of the full choir. The work made a lively impression that resulted in the composer being called for and enthusiastically applauded on his appearance on the platform. (emphasis added)

This review—nowhere cited in the Delius scholarly literature—was not published in the London *Times*, nor in any other English newspapers and journals on file at the British Library's Newspaper Library in London, which I visited in September 1993. A search through leading American music journals was also unproductive. Its source remains at present a mystery.

In contrast to the negative or at best lukewarm English criticisms of *Appalachia* quoted in the Delius literature, the description above is sympathetic, even enthusiastic. The reviewer's judgment—"a work of remarkable emotional power . . . touching on the mysterious"—allows us to understand the lasting impression the strange music made on Percy Grainger and Thomas Beecham. (Both men were in the audience that evening and came under the composer's spell, Beecham for the first time.) Equally important, the commentary solves a long-standing puzzle in the Delius story: the geographical source of *Appalachia*'s slave song. It came not from the tobacco stemmeries of Danville, Virginia, as is generally accepted, but from the St. Johns River in northern Florida. Who but Delius himself, in London for the important premiere, could have provided reviewers with particular background about the tune? This conclusion seems incontestable. (The composer/critic Robin Legge's review of the same concert in the *London Daily Telegraph* of November 23, 1907, also makes this point: *Appalachia* "consists of some fourteen orchestral variations, with short choral finale, upon a genuine slave song sung nightly outside Mr. Delius's house what time he lived in Florida as orange-grower, the singer being a quondam slave.")

The *Post*'s publication of this review becomes more intriguing when we consider that Delius's name was unknown in America in 1907, except to a select few, such as the anonymous "scholarly musician" of Houston. The review of *Appalachia* awakened such interest among local musicians that another article about its composer appeared in the *Post* on December 29, two weeks later. Despite obvious errors, the newspaper's critic—probably Mrs. Wille Hutcheson, the newspaper's regular music critic—was able to shed light on the composer's connection to the South in general—and to Houston in particular:

Again the Author of "Appalachia"

The mention in these columns two weeks ago of Alfred [sic] Delius and his American opera [sic] has called out from several of his compatriots residing now in Houston much interesting matter concerning this English composer's musical career.

Among the items brought to the editor's notice the following data hold special local interest:

The first concert of Delius' music in England was given in April, 1899, in St. James hall, London. The program was made up of excerpts from his operas "Koanga" and "Zarathustra." On this occasion a certain innovation introduced by Delius into orchestral music may be attributed to the influences of his many years' residence in the Southern States of America. This innovation was the use of banjos in addition to [the] regular [Wagnerian] ring orchestra. . . .

When Delius gave his "Koanga" in London the American banjoist, Alfred Cammeyer, was playing at the Alhambra music hall, so he was pressed into service. This was the first time the banjo had ever appeared as an orchestral instrument. The London critics pronounced Delius' music that of the future and predicted for him a great career. Which prediction seems at present about to be fulfilled.

Alfred Hertz, whom Houstonians remember as leader of the Metropolitan orchestra for the performance of "Parsifal" here, made his debut as a conductor at this same concert of Delius' music in 1899. And it was through his performance at that same affair that he obtained his engagement with the management of the New York Metropolitan. The name of a gentleman who is now one of our own fellow citizens appeared also on that Delius program. Mr. Douglas Powell, choirmaster of the First Presbyterian church, sang the "Mitternacht Lied" from "Zarathustra."[26]

The second of the *Post's* articles on *Appalachia* introduces two interesting paradoxes. When Alfred Hertz conducted the Metropolitan Opera Company in Heinrich Conried's staging of *Parsifal* on April 22, 1905, Houston had for weeks been anticipating a musical milestone. It was to be the "event of the season," the *Post* proclaimed on April 21, citing the city's outbreak of "Parsifalitis." (To enlighten the public properly, on April 16 the paper had allotted an entire page to the leitmotifs of Wagner's "Sacred Consecration Festival.") Thomas Ward was surely among those attending the momentous

event, for in early 1905 he was still much involved in the city's musical activities. How ironic that, unknown to him, he would have been watching the conductor of the first major concert of Frederick Delius's music!

It is also an extraordinary happenstance that Douglas Powell, the first singer of Delius's setting from Nietzsche's *Also sprach Zarathustra*, was in 1907 earning his living at a church only a few blocks from Ward's residence. A "thoroughly equipped musician" who, according to the *Post* of December 29, 1907, had recently settled in Houston, Powell would soon establish a reputation as "the Gibraltar of our home musicians" and guest-conduct the visiting Chicago Symphony Orchestra and a large local chorus in Rossini's *Stabat Mater*, an event lavishly reported in the *Post* of May 3, 1908. Powell also conducted the yearly concert of the Festival Association, a combination of choirs from several Texas cities. In Houston's small circle of church musicians, Thomas Ward would probably have known Powell and may have learned firsthand from him about Delius's rapid artistic progress after Florida.

But who was responsible for the local publication of the *Appalachia* review and who posted it to America? Surely it was not Powell who contacted the paper. In 1907 his repertoire as soloist and choirmaster at Houston's First Presbyterian Church (given in the Sunday newspapers) reveals nothing reflecting the tastes of a "scholarly musician." From the context of the second article, Powell seems clearly to have been merely one of the Englishmen "called out from several of his compatriots," as the paper phrased it. Nor is it likely that Delius would have interrupted a busy social schedule in London to dispatch the review to Powell, a passing professional acquaintance of eight years earlier.

But if *Thomas F. Ward* were that "scholarly musician"—he was known for his "large library"—our assessment of his relationship to Delius would need substantial revision. Is it possible that Delius himself sent the appreciative review to Ward as a souvenir of their Florida past and that the two men reestablished contact after Ward left St. Leo? This theory opens up a host of unanswerable questions. Why would Delius have concealed from Philip Heseltine information about Ward's later life, preferring to paint for him the romantic picture of a monk dying young in tropical Florida rather than the realistic one of a middle-aged musician in a provincial American city? Why would Delius want to revise the truth and burn his bridges to this part of his past? One fact remains: All correspondence of Ward to Delius has disappeared, whether it originated in the 1880s, when Ward definitely wrote letters to

him, or in the 1900s, when any exchanges would be conjectural. Perhaps later communications to Delius were among the many letters destroyed by Delius's widow Jelka shortly after his death in 1934.[27] Without additional documentation, the complete relationship of Ward and Delius cannot be known and will remain a puzzle forever unsolved. Whatever the case, the tantalizing clues of the *Houston Post* abruptly ceased, the "Author of Appalachia" never appeared in the city's press again during Ward's lifetime, and the "Appalachia affair" soon passed from public memory.

✦ At the time Houstonians were discussing *Appalachia*, Ward had already stopped performing publicly. There seems to be only one explanation for his withdrawal: symptoms of progressive tuberculosis perceptible to anyone frequently in his company. The condition, of necessity, had to be kept private and unobtrusive.

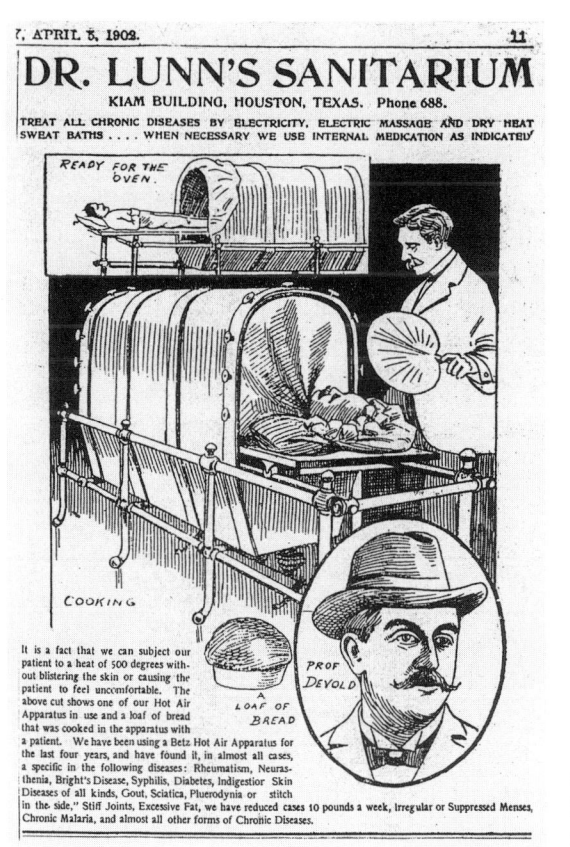

Advertisement for Dr. Lunn's Sanitarium. (*Houston Chronicle*, April 5, 1902.)

Except to the quack advertisers of instant cures, tuberculosis was looked upon with little sympathy in Houston in the early 1900s. (A typical advertisement in the *Chronicle* of April 5, 1902—for "Dr. Lunn's Sanitarium"— promises to "treat all chronic diseases by electricity, electric massage and dry heat sweat baths. . . . When necessary we use internal medication.") The humanitarian Anti-Tuberculosis League attempted to improve the welfare of consumptives but made little dent in the city's prejudice against them. Houston looked toward a healthy and prosperous future, not to one clouded by sickness and chronic disease, which, with clever local politics, could be hidden from public view. Pleading in 1912 (the year of Ward's death) for the first tuberculosis sanitarium within city limits, the League acknowledged the size and gravity of the tuberculosis problem but had no success in persuading the citizenry that such an establishment would be anything but a "menace to the health of the other residents of the city," an institution that would turn Houston, into "a rendezvous and a resort for consumptives." The answer to the problem, said the League, in the pages of the *Post* the year Ward died, lay in the creation of a good facility "reasonably accessible and yet sufficiently removed from the crowded centers of population":

> At present the indigent advanced consumptive must either remain in his own home, enter the common wards of a general hospital or go to the county farm, in either of which places those around him not similarly afflicted are daily and hourly exposed to the infection. Is this right? . . . Our effort is to cure as many incipients as possible . . . but by all means to protect the well people, or those ill from disease other than tuberculosis, from the advanced consumptive. Every case in Houston who has been or is now being visited by the tuberculosis nurse has not only expressed a willingness but an intense desire to be removed from their homes that they might no longer be a *menace* to other members of the family. (October 20, 1912, emphasis added)

According to newspaper headlines, one physician, Dr. E. P. Daviss, replying publicly to this proposal, called such a sanitarium "Out of Place in Houston" and a "Grave Mistake" that would greatly increase the tubercular colony. Describing the unfavorable climate of the city in the *Post*, he offered the view of most Houstonians:

> Many patients, returning to Houston, have within a few months or a single winter relapsed into their former condition, though continuing treatment.

. . . We are assured that Houston now has at least 900 [consumptives], all of whom are now such a *menace* to the health of others. . . . It should be rational and proper to arrange temporary quarters at the poor farm for segregating special charges of the city and county poor, but a tubercular sanitarium should have climatic and hygienic surroundings not attainable here. (October 27, 1912, emphasis added)

In the discussion of Houston's consumptives, the word "menace" occurs often in the public discourse.

Ward's practical solution to these pressures was simple: to avoid becoming ostracized, he yielded to social pressure and loosened the bond between his music and his religion. In the years that remained to him, he continued to teach quietly and to work as a little-noticed orchestral musician. He kept to himself until illness and poverty overwhelmed him.

But the close bond between the man and the Catholic Church remained intact. He was fortunate that someone of Father Hennessy's caliber was present to hear his dying confession, to give him the last rites of the Church, and to preside at his burial. On the day of his death in May 1912, Thomas F. Ward left little behind but his "large library" (perhaps with his own compositions) and a few dependable friends. All have long since vanished.

⇥ Epilogue

"After night has gone comes the day, the dark shadows will fade away."
—Frederick Delius, *Appalachia*

On November 1, 1988, All Saints' Day, I found myself at the old Holy Cross Cemetery in Houston. In this rundown part of the city, most of the commercial signs and graffiti were in Spanish; two miles to the south the skyscrapers of modern Houston glistened across the Buffalo Bayou. Anticipating my visit, cemetery caretakers Ron Smith and Ernest MacMillan had located Ward's unmarked grave with its numbered lot stone, long covered over, and they took me to it. It was an absurdly beautiful summer-like autumn day; squirrels scurried among the moss-hung trees, shrubbery, and flowers in the absolute silence. I sat on the grass and on my Walkman listened to Delius's *Life's Dance* with its theme of struggle and joy in existence; then to "La Calinda" and "By the River" from the *Florida Suite,* with their depiction of youth, tranquility, and solitude in Florida. "La Calinda" had never sounded so lovely as in this, its natural southern setting; and finally, to *Appalachia:* "Oh Honey, I am going down the river in the morning." The circle seemed to have become complete, more than thirty years after Mr. Hugh had casually mentioned the name of Thomas F. Ward.

On the next day, All Souls' Day, I returned. A mass in Spanish and English for the unknown dead was being celebrated in the cemetery, in the unexpected absence of the bishop, by Rev. Stephen Horn of the Christ the King Church. He spoke about the many lives who have gone on before us whose names have been lost in the sand—who have not been remembered, though their lives have touched others. He said that we are here but for a fleeting moment in nature (Delius?), but eternity lies before us (Ward?). Afterward, I took the priest to Thomas Ward's grave, where I had placed flowers and two

Grave site of Thomas F. Ward, Holy Cross Cemetery, Houston, 1988. (Photo by Sabine Matthes.)

roses, one from me and the other in Sister Mary Albert's name, and he blessed the site. In an inarticulate way, I told him of my long quest and of how I had attempted to find out who this uncommon man was and what had happened to him. Thinking of his sermon, I told him about a forgotten but meaningful life and about a sequence of events that the person in the grave had helped set in motion many years ago in Florida. I wanted him to know what it meant to me and that it was the end of a long, long search. He smiled and said, "Now you know."

At that moment I did know that Ward's had not been a life of failure, unless one equates the absence of fame and wealth and family with failure. Then, if so, is it not true that a man who fails well is greater than one who succeeds badly? Had he not given generously of himself? As Merton wrote, "We do not exist for ourselves alone, and it is only when we are fully convinced of this fact that we begin to love ourselves properly and thus also love others . . . desiring to live, accepting life as a very great gift and a great good, not because of what it gives us, but because of what it enables us to give to others."[1] It was this peaceful state of acceptance that had been his real goal at St. Leo. As Sister Mary Albert reflected in a note to me on July 11, 1991: "God allowed Thomas Ward [after leaving Florida] to arrive at a much healthier point of self-acceptance. Ward had concealed the truth of his birth but was now freed to release *all* his grief and move ahead with his life. In that newfound freedom a lessening of need for neurotic defense would follow. In mid-life he was able to make his way, use his talents, and cultivate personal relationships suited to personality." In Houston, Texas, he could conduct his life positively without the guilt that had long followed him.

On April 28, 1912, in the year that he was revising *Life's Dance* and composing the pantheistic *Song of the High Hills*, and less than two weeks before the day his teacher Ward was buried, the pupil Delius wrote to Philip Heseltine, whose words about the meeting of Delius and Ward began this story and my quest: "Christianity is paralysing—If one is sincere it utterly unfits one for life. . . . The moment you chuck all this rot overboard Life becomes interesting—wonderful."[2] I wondered again why fate (or providence if you will) had brought fame to the blasphemous student and oblivion to the devout teacher. There is no answer to this question. As Sister Mary Albert told me on my return from Houston, the thing that matters most is that Delius was given the gift of communicating intense beauty to other human beings. This gift, called genius, needed only to be brought into focus by someone with the right spirit, Thomas F. Ward, in the right place, Florida.

I began my search for Ward under the powerful spell of Delius's *Appalachia*, and its refrains followed me everywhere. Shortly before Delius returned to Solano Grove in the spring of 1897 to learn of his teacher's "death," he composed the short, in some ways immature, *American Rhapsody*, in which in addition to the "Appalachia" theme, we can hear the combined tunes of "Dixie" and "Yankee Doodle," the latter song's rhythms given after a slow introduction and its melody heard nostalgically at the ending. It is doubtful whether

Florida coquina stone memorial placed on Thomas F. Ward's grave site, July 27, 1993. (Photo by Don Gillespie.)

"Yankee Doodle" meant anything at all to Delius, who spent almost his entire American sojourn in the Deep South, where, less than twenty years distant in time from the Civil War, the tune could hardly have been popular. Can we perhaps hear in it, not just a work of naïve juvenilia, but also a tribute to Ward, the "Yankee" who came to town—to Jacksonville, Florida—and influenced deeply Delius's own future? Such musings are, of course, distant from the objective concerns of musicology.

It was Delius's great fortune that his artistic life was framed at its beginning and near its end by strong, devout Catholics: Thomas Ward and Eric Fenby. One added discipline to the confidence and raw talent of youth; the other nurtured the late masterpieces of old age. Fenby, on learning of the circumstances of Ward's death, wrote to me on March 6, 1989: "Delius would have been shocked, though perhaps not surprised to hear of his neglected fate. I am glad that now I can pray from my heart with confidence for his soul."

After the many years of my pursuit, Thomas F. Ward has kept his strange aura. He had lived a quarter-century past the time music history had as-

signed for his demise. I had discovered many things about him, but I had not taken away his mystery. I realized that those who are destined for greatness sometimes owe unpayable spiritual debts to those who are not. Did my quest mean anything else? Religion aside, perhaps Delius was wrong and Ward was right. The deepest sensations are not transient. The passage of time does not erode the fundamental values that lie beyond our sensual experiences.

Another person realized these things also, but in a much more profoundly religious way than I. Like Eric Fenby, Sister Mary Albert Lussier had also prayed for Ward, on behalf of the Sisters of St. Joseph, for whom not even a century's passage had erased the solicitude felt for one in their care: "The living pray for the dead; also, those already in God's eternal presence do pray for the living. How consoling!" Perhaps the spirits of Thomas F. Ward and Frederick Delius reside somewhere in those remarks. I hope so.

The St. Johns River from Solano Grove at sunset. (Photo by Robert Beckhard.)

→ Notes

Introduction

1. Chop, *Frederick Delius, Monographien moderner Musiker*, vol. 2.
2. Hill, "Frederick Delius" (emphasis added).
3. Heseltine, *Frederick Delius*, 17–18, 21.
4. Fenby, *Delius as I Knew Him*, 168–69.
5. Ibid., 167–68, 170.
6. See Fenby, *Delius*, 17, 20.
7. Fenby, "On Delius in Florida," 5.
8. For an account of Delius's stay in Virginia, see Mary Cahill, *Delius in Danville*.
9. The volume is now at the Swisher Library, Jacksonville University.
10. Clare Delius, *Frederick Delius: Memories of My Brother*, 74.
11. Jahoda, *Road to Samarkand*, 50–55.
12. Burnett, *Florida's Past: People and Events that Shaped the State*, 43.
13. Deems Taylor, *Of Men and Music*, 35–36.
14. Typescript of a talk on Delius by Kathryn S. Lawson, archivist of the St. Augustine Historical Society, given to the St. Cecilia Society, St. Augustine, Florida, Mar. 26, 1940 (St. Augustine Historical Society).

Chapter 1: Brooklyn

1. This memo, now at the Swisher Library, Jacksonville University, is an appendage to Mrs. Richmond's description of a visit to Solano Grove in 1939.
2. Meany, *By Railway or Rainbow*, 74ff.
3. Arthur Hutchings states that Ward is "the older man by a decade" in *Delius*, 17. In his *Frederick Delius*, Heseltine places him "some nine years older" (40); at the time of Heseltine's writing, however, Delius thought his birth year was 1863. Sir Thomas Beecham believed that in 1884 "Ward was just over thirty," about eight years older than Delius (*Frederick Delius*, 28). Fenby states in *Delius as I Knew Him* that Ward was Delius's "senior by a few months" (168).

4. Keany, *A Brief Historical Sketch of the Roman Catholic Orphan Asylum of Brooklyn*, 9.

5. New York State Census of 1865, Kings County, Brooklyn, part 1 of the 4th Ward, p. 28 (State Supreme Court Building, Brooklyn). Censuses taken in Brooklyn on the dates below give Ward's age as follows: New York State Census of 1865 (June 21, 1865): 10 [b. 1855]; U.S. Census of 1870 (July 1, 1870): 14 [b. 1856]; New York State Census of 1875 (July 2–4, 1875): 18 [b. 1857]; U.S. Census of 1880 (June 3, 1880): 24 [b. 1856].

6. U.S. Census of 1870, Kings County, Brooklyn, Ward 6, p. 41.

7. U.S. Census of 1860, Kings County, 2d District, 12th Ward, p. 96 (State Supreme Court Building, Brooklyn); Brooklyn Directory of 1860–61. The perils of using bibliographic tools are herein illustrated. The ink entry I found in 1986 in the original census book is faded but legible. It is unreadable in government microfilms of the 1860 census, and it is not to be found at all in a two-volume *Index to the 1860 U.S. Census of Brooklyn and Queens*, published in 1987. Had I attempted to solve this riddle in 1988 rather than in 1986, I would not have found the family of Thomas Ward.

8. Martha S. Hendren, Office of the Abbot, Belmont Abbey, to the author, June 2, 1986.

9. Belmont Abbey Archives.

10. Bishop McDonnell to Rev. Hintemeyer, July 7, 1894, Belmont Abbey Archives. The letters and "testimony" from Maryhelp Abbey have not survived in the Archives of the Diocese of Brooklyn.

11. Belmont Abbey Archives.

12. Sharp, *Priests and Parishes of the Diocese of Brooklyn* (1820–1944). Rev. Thomas F. Ward (1844–1898), the well-known Catholic scholar and pastor of the Church of St. Charles Borromeo in Brooklyn Heights, listed herein, is not related to the orphan Ward.

13. Death certificate no. 6254, Municipal Archives, New York City.

14. Hueppe, *The Radiant Light: A History of St. John's College*, 16–18.

15. Program of the Second Annual Exhibition, June 24, 1872 (St. John's University Archives).

16. Ibid.

17. Program of the Third Annual Exhibition of St. John's College, June 24, 1873 (St. John's University Archives).

18. *Brooklyn Eagle*, Apr. 11, 1873; May 3, 1876.

19. Ibid., Mar. 30, 1874.

20. "Aus den Inskriptionsbüchern der Hochschule geht nicht hervor, dass Thomas F. Ward in Leipzig studiert haben könnte." Christine Piech, Hochschule für Musik, "Felix Mendelssohn Bartholdy," Leipzig, to author, Apr. 12, 1989.

21. Hughes, *Contemporary American Composers*, 344–45.

22. "Stories of Old Brooklyn," *Brooklyn Eagle*, Dec. 30, 1931.

23. *Brooklyn Eagle*, Dec. 7, 1882; Apr. 13, 1875.

24. Odell, *Annals of the New York Stage*, 9:224.

25. John Loretz to Emma Thursby, Jan. 10, 1883 (Emma Thursby Collection, New-York Historical Society).

26. New York State Census of 1860, 11th Ward, 2d District: Age 20.

27. Palmer, *History of Hollywood*, 143.

28. Death certificate no. 12-023751, State of California. The *Brooklyn Eagle*'s feature article on Loretz, "Stories of Old Brooklyn" (Dec. 30, 1931), erroneously gives 1908 as the year of his death.

29. *Brooklyn Eagle*, Jan. 29, 1873.

30. New York State Census of 1875, Kings County, 1st Election District of the 24th Ward (State Supreme Court Building, Brooklyn).

31. Offergeld, "Gottschalk and Company," notes to New World Records NW-257, "The Wind Demon and Other Mid-19th-Century Piano Music," Ivan Davis, pianist.

32. Mason, *Memories of a Musical Life*, 206.

33. *Catholic Review*, Feb. 19, 1881. The famous Athenaeum, on the corner of Clinton Street and Atlantic Avenue has long been replaced by commercial buildings and is now the site of a supermarket.

34. Ibid., Nov. 29, 1878.

35. *Brooklyn Tablet*, Mar. 29, 1958.

36. *Memorial of the Golden Jubilee of the Rev. Sylvester Malone*, 29.

37. Phone conversation with Dr. Mary Wolfe, Office of Catholic Education, July 10, 1986.

38. *Brooklyn Eagle*, Dec. 24, 1882.

39. *Memorial of the Golden Jubilee*, 46, 50.

Chapter 2: Jacksonville and St. Augustine

1. *Webb's Jacksonville and Consolidated Directory*, 1886, 222. No city directories exist for the years 1883–85.

2. *Richards' Jacksonville City Directory*, 1887, 105.

3. *Webb's Historical, Industrial and Biographical Florida*, 1885, 173.

4. Ibid., 159. By 1886 the store had moved from Ocean Street to a more stable location at 48 East Bay Street next to the post office (see also *Webb's Jacksonville*).

5. Delius to Jelka Rosen (Apr. 1897), in *Delius: A Life in Letters*, ed. Lionel Carley, 1:113–14.

6. Hearn, *Leaves from the Diary of an Impressionist*, 38, 41–42.

7. Heseltine, "Some Notes on Delius and His Music."

8. Jahoda, "The Music-Maker of Solano Grove," 264–68.

9. "Notebook I," in *A Catalogue of the Compositions of Frederick Delius*, ed. Robert Threlfall, 196.

10. Carley to author, Jan. 29, 1990.

11. Threlfall to author, Feb. 1, 1990.

12. The Grainger Museum at the University of Melbourne possesses another document linked to Delius's study with Ward: an elementary contrapuntal study labeled by Eric Fenby, "An early counterpoint exercise written by Delius for Thomas Ward on the plantation in Florida." Written in neither Delius's nor Ward's hand, its association with Solano Grove seems to me doubtful.

13. For a more skeptical view of the "chance meeting" of Ward and Delius, see Randel, "More on that Long-Lost Mistress," 10–11.

14. Randel, "Delius in America," 155.

15. "Piano Used by Composer Placed in Delius Cottage," Florida Times-Union, Nov. 30, 1965; see also, Charles Hofmann, "He Set Florida to Music."

16. Jahoda, "Music-Maker," 264.

17. "Glimpses of Life in City 75 Years Ago Given by Bartola Genovar, Aged 93," St. Augustine Record, July 30, 1939.

18. Grainger, "The Personality of Frederick Delius," 122.

19. Randel, "More on that Long-Lost Mistress," 11.

20. "'Fairy Elves' by Thos. F. Ward," from Frederick Delius's "Red, Leather-Bound Pocket Notebook" (Grainger Museum, Melbourne). The handwriting is neither Ward's nor Delius's. I am indebted to Roger J. Buckley for this source.

21. Danese, One Hundred and Twenty-Five Years, 1854–1979: A History of the Church of the Immaculate Conception, 6.

22. Ibid., 9.

23. Florida Times-Union, Dec. 25, 1885.

24. Ibid., Mar. 20, 1887. In cultural matters, the newspaper preferred French whenever possible!

25. Grier Moffatt Williams, "A History of Music in Jacksonville, Florida, from 1822 to 1922," 137–39.

26. The Times-Union observed that Florence Keep "by the way has been entirely educated in Europe" ("Some Society Gossip," Apr. 5, 1885).

27. Florida Times-Union, Mar. 20, 1887.

28. Ibid., Apr. 13, 1886. The program's contents were printed on this date.

29. Ibid., May 14, 1887. The polonaise was not the now-famous op. 53 in A-flat, but the relatively easy op. 26, no. 1 in C-sharp minor.

30. Typescript of an interview by Rose Shepherd, June 6, 1938 (Swisher Library). Frederikke Mordt-Mencke (Mrs. Andrew Mencke) was the sister of Jutta Belle-Ranske, Delius's neighbor and friend at Solano Grove.

31. Typescript summary of a phone interview by Martha B. Richmond, May 28, 1945 (Jacksonville Public Library).

32. Williams, "History of Music," 74ff.

33. Florida Times-Union, Apr. 8, 1887.

34. Ibid., Feb. 26 and 28, 1887.

35. Ibid., Apr. 8, 1887.

36. Popular Health Resorts of the South, 136.

37. Bishop John Moore to "Dr. Pace," Sept. 12, 1888 (Archives of the Diocese of St. Augustine, Mandarin, Fla.).

38. Lanier, Florida: Its Scenery, Climate, and History, 39, 65–67, 216.

39. For further information on Flagler's hotels, see Chandler, Henry Flagler; and Nolan, Fifty Feet in Paradise.

40. "St. Augustine Notes," *Florida Times-Union*, Apr. 8, 1887. See also Harvey, *St. Augustine and St. Johns County: A Pictorial History*, 86.

41. Advertisement in *Popular Health Resorts*.

42. *Florida Times-Union*, July 30, 1887.

43. "The Old Cathedral," *Florida Times-Union*, June 12, 1887 (by "I. W.").

44. I am indebted to Joseph Manucy of St. Augustine for bringing to my attention the fact that Ward was the author of this announcement. In a letter to Martha B. Richmond in 1954, Manucy described his excitement at finding an old newspaper establishing a connection between Delius's teacher and the services in the convent of the Sisters of St. Joseph, whose school and chapel he had attended as a boy (Manucy to Richmond, Apr. 2, 1954 [Jacksonville Public Library]). During my visits on March 5 and August 16, 1986, he recalled this detail with certainty: it was the year of his mother's birth, "the year of the big fire." At first I doubted his memory. I could find no mention of Ward's name at the St. Augustine Historical Society, even in the microfilm of the *St. Johns County Weekly* announcement of April 16, 1887. On the microfilm at the University of Florida in Gainesville, however, "T. F. Ward" stands out clearly, verifying Manucy's account. On the copy at the St. Augustine Historical Society, the name had been obliterated by a defect in the film—a matter of sheer chance.

45. *St. Augustine Weekly News*, Jan. 31, 1889.

46. Chandler, *Henry Flagler*, 94.

47. *Elliott's Florida Encyclopedia or Pocket Directory*, 234.

48. Advertisement for the Carleton Hotel in *Popular Health Resorts*.

49. Red leather-bound ledger book of the Carleton Hotel, Dec. 12, 1881, Sanford to Aug. 31, 1888, St. Augustine, pp. 79, 145 (in possession of Marjorie A. Blaskower, Greenbrae, California). It seems logical to assume that Ward's music lessons would have been given to members of the Teahen family. I am grateful to Marjorie A. Blaskower, W. M. Teahen's great-granddaughter, for her own intensive analysis of the Carleton's ledgers and for access to her family archives.

50. Red leather-bound cash book of the Carleton Hotel, Feb. 21, 1887, to Jan. 29, 1891, p. 100.

51. W. M. Teahen's bound servants time book, Oct. 1876 to Apr. 1889, pp. 39, 58.

52. Ledger of the Carleton Hotel, p. 108. Dr. Webb later founded the St. Augustine Historical Society.

53. This hotel was eventually renamed the "Teahen House" (conversation with Marjorie A. Blaskower).

54. W. M. Teahen's bank book, the Lyman Bank of Sanford, Florida, p. 6.

55. Old financial records discovered in 1994 in storage at the Cathedral now prove conclusively that Ward continued to be employed intermittently as organist and occasional choir director during the two-year period from October 1887 to December 1889, earning approximately twenty-five dollars monthly (Cathedral cash book, 21–81, Archives, Diocese of St. Augustine, Mandarin, Fla.).

56. *Orlando City Directory of 1891* (Orange County History Museum).

Chapter 3: St. Leo Monastery

1. St. Leo Military College catalogue, 1892–93 (St. Leo Archives).

2. Lucie Vannevar, "With the Benedictine Sisters," *Sanford Journal* (written late Jan. 1891), Holy Name Priory Archives Scrapbook. See also, Horgan, *Pioneer College: The Centennial History of Saint Leo College, Saint Leo Abbey, and Holy Name Priory*, 57. Historical background on St. Leo Monastery is based principally upon this source.

3. Merton, *No Man Is an Island*, 145, 74.

4. *Sadlier's Catholic Directory*, 1889–90.

5. Horgan, *Pioneer College*, 568.

6. Ibid., 83, 87, 130.

7. Dressman, ed. *St. Leo Golden Jubilee, 1890–1940*, 22.

8. *Florida Times-Union*, Apr. 15; Sept. 21, 1890.

9. Horgan, *Pioneer College*, 34–35, 67.

10. *Sanford Journal*, Sept. 26, 1891, from James J. Horgan's "Preparatory Notes." I am indebted to Professor Horgan, who allowed me to use his chronological outline for *Pioneer College*. His extensive notes (herein cited as "Preparatory Notes") include lengthy extracts from the diary ("chronology") of Father Benedict Roth, O.S.B., and are based upon materials in the St. Leo Archives, to which I was denied access after 1986.

11. St. Leo Military College catalogue, 1891–92.

12. Horgan, *Pioneer College*, 210–11.

13. The photograph appears in ibid., 70.

14. McKay, "Pioneer Florida."

15. Frater Paul [Thomas F. Ward], "Class Mementoes of the Cardinal Virtues" (St. Leo Archives, courtesy of James J. Horgan).

16. [Thomas F. Ward], "Observer," *San Antonio Herald*, Apr. 15, 1892 (St. Leo Abbey scrapbook no. 1, p. 40, St. Leo Archives). On the clipping, next to the word "Observer," Father Benedict wrote in ink: "Fr. Paul" (courtesy of James J. Horgan).

17. A student who came to St. Leo in 1934 to improve his English was the entertainer Desi Arnaz.

18. Frater Paul [Thomas F. Ward], "Class Mementoes, 1892–93" (St. Leo Abbey scrapbook no. 1, p. 70).

19. St. Leo Military College catalogue, 1895–96. Ward was studying "First Theology." The *Catholic Directory* of 1896 lists him as a "Professor of Philosophy."

20. The certificate, dated January 18, 1893, is located in one of the St. Leo Abbey's scrapbooks.

21. Conversation with Professor Roger Landroth, Baruch College of Business, New York City, Oct. 17, 1988.

22. [Thomas F. Ward], "Observer," *San Antonio Herald*, Apr. 15, 1892.

23. *St. Leo's Magazine* 7, no. 1 (1919–20): 15 (St. Leo Archives). Bass are still called "trout" in Georgia and Florida.

24. Horgan, *Pioneer College*, 134.

25. St. Leo Military College catalogues, 1891–92, 1892–93, and 1895–96.

26. Horgan, *Pioneer College*, 221–22. Shabaker, who arrived the same month as Ward, later became a missionary in Cuba.

27. Ibid., 220.

28. Ibid., 223–24, 35.

29. St. Leo Military College catalogue, 1891–92. Musical selections for the commencement exercises are to be found in the annual college catalogues, which appeared at the end of the academic year.

30. San Antonio *Florida Staats-Zeitung*, June 25, 1896 (P. K. Yonge Library, Gainesville). Translated by author.

31. This translation was provided by Professor Seth Benardete, Department of Classics, New York University.

32. Grainger, "About Delius."

33. St. Leo Military College catalogue, 1896–97.

34. Grainger, "The Genius of Frederick Delius."

35. William H. Humiston, Program Notes for Delius's Piano Concerto in C Minor, Philharmonic Society of New York, November 26, 1915.

36. *St. Leo's Magazine* 4, no. 4 (1917): 103 (St. Leo Archives).

37. *The Benedictines in Florida*.

38. Roth chronology, Apr. 26, 1893 ("Preparatory Notes").

39. Martha S. Hendren, Office of the Abbot, Belmont Abbey, to author, July 17, 1986.

40. Minutes of the Independent Priory [of St. Leo], Oct. 7, 1894, Father Louis Panoch, Secretary (St. Leo Archives).

41. Horgan to author, Oct. 19, 1989.

42. Memorandum of Father Charles Mohr, Roth chronology, July 14, 1895 ("Preparatory Notes").

43. Minutes of the Independent Priory, Aug. 31, 1895.

44. Conversation with Father Richard Harnett, S.J., Tampa, Aug. 20, 1986.

45. Sister Mary Albert Lussier to author, Dec. 11, 1986.

46. Conversation with Father Leo Schlosser, St. Leo Abbey, Aug. 18, 1986.

47. Conversation with Father Harry M. Culkin, Brooklyn, New York, July 29, 1988.

48. From a monastery scrapbook, St. Leo Archives (courtesy of Father Henry Riffle, O.S.B.).

Chapter 4: St. Leo and Tampa

1. *The Jesuits in Florida: Fifty Golden Years, 1889–1939*, 12–13.

2. Ibid.

3. Kenny, "Jesuits in Our Southland, 1566–1946."

4. Lucy O'Brien, *Sacred Heart Parish Centennial, 1860–1960*, 19, 21.

5. McGrath, "Man of Vision as Seen by a Friend."

6. House diary of St. Louis Church, Tampa (Loyola University Archives, New Orleans).

7. Minutes of the Independent Priory [of St. Leo], Oct. 21, 1896 (St. Leo Archives).

8. First letter of Thomas F. Ward to Father Charles Mohr, Oct. 21, 1896 (St. Leo Archives). The italic words were underlined in blue pencil by Father Charles; the word "Architectural" was crossed out by Ward.

9. Letter of Thomas F. Ward [Frater Placidus] to Rev. Benedict Roth, [Oct. 21, 1896] (St. Leo Archives).

10. Undated memo of Father Charles Mohr (St. Leo Archives).

11. Merton, No Man Is an Island, 120–21.

12. Minutes of the Independent Priory, Oct. 21, 1896 (St. Leo Archives).

13. Merton, No Man Is an Island, 156–57.

14. Second letter of Thomas F. Ward to Father Charles Mohr, Oct. 21, 1896 (St. Leo Archives).

15. Bentley, "Tampa's Old Hotels Seem to Live on in Many Ways."

16. Third letter of Thomas F. Ward to Father Charles Mohr, Oct. 23, 1896 (St. Leo Archives).

17. Postcard of Mary F. Ward, Nov. 15, 1896 (St. Leo Archives, courtesy of Father Henry Riffle).

18. Brooklyn Catholic Review, July 18, 1874; July 16, 1873.

19. House diary of St. Louis Church, book 2, 76–78 (Loyola University Archives). The Jesuit Archives at Grand Coteau were transferred to New Orleans in 1988.

20. Threlfall, Catalogue of the Compositions, 77.

21. New Orleans Daily Picayune, Nov. 3, 1896. A photograph of the Florida and its schedule appear in Prince, Atlantic Coast Line Railroad Steam Locomotives, Ships and History, 47–48.

Chapter 5: Louisiana and Texas

1. Musical America 18, no. 23 (1913): 124.

2. [Abbot Leo Haid], St. Mary's College, Belmont, N.C., to Rev. Charles Mohr, Nov. 2, 1896 (St. Leo Archives). The letter is incomplete and unsigned.

3. Thomson and Meador, Shreveport: A Photographic Remembrance, 1873–1949, 20–21.

4. St. Leo Archives. Emphasis added. Ward's original letter is lost.

5. Ibid.

6. Ibid. Translated from the Latin by Father Gerald Barbarito, Office of the Chancery, Diocese of Brooklyn.

7. Isaac Borocz, O.S.B., Secretary to the Abbot Primate, St. Anselm of the City [of Rome], to author, Dec. 8, 1988.

8. Beckman, Kansas Monks: A History of St. Benedict's Abbey, 156–57.

9. Rev. Gilbert F. Wolters, O.S.B., archivist of St. Benedict's Abbey, to author, Oct. 25, 1988.

10. Phone conversation with Brother Malachy McCarthy, O.S.B., St. Anselm Abbey, Manchester, N.H., Sept. 14, 1988.

11. The Diocese of Alexandria, formerly the Diocese of Nachitoches, has no record of Ward's dispensation in its archive. The cathedral, however, was not required to

record a dispensation unless the person involved was a priest (phone conversation with Monsignor Julius Walle, archivist, Diocese of Alexandria, Oct. 12, 1988).

12. U.S. Census of 1910, enumeration district 92, Ward 3, Houston, Texas.

13. John P. Murphy, director of Vital Records, Texas Department of Health, to author, Dec. 8, 1988.

14. Conversation with Monsignor Teodoro de la Torre at Annunciation Church, Houston, Texas, Nov. 1, 1988. Ten pages are missing from the original book, now in the Archives of the Diocese of Galveston-Houston.

15. See obituary of Anton Diehl in *Houston Press*, Nov. 6, 1952; *New Encyclopedia of Texas*, ed. Ellis A. Davis and Edwin H. Grobe, s.v. "Diehl, Anton."

16. *Houstonian*, Nov. 12, 1904, features a typical advertisement.

17. *New Encyclopedia of Texas*, ed. Davis and Grobe, s.v. "Diehl, Anton."

18. "Sacred Heart Catholic [Church]," *Houston Daily Post*, Feb. 8, 1914.

19. Phone conversation with Lisa May, archivist of the Diocese of Galveston-Houston, Feb. 25, 1993.

20. Music critic Carl Cunningham's article about Ward (based on my discoveries) stirred no older Houstonians' memories. See his "Searching for Clues to the Last Days of One Thomas F. Ward."

21. Roussel, *The Houston Symphony Orchestra, 1913–1971*, 15–16.

22. *New Grove Dictionary of Music and Musicians*, 6th ed., s.v. "Gaul, Alfred (Robert)."

23. Preface to the vocal score of *The Holy City* (New York: G. Schirmer, 1901). The work remains in print today—a steady seller.

24. Sam T. Swinford, "Musical Houston, 1901–1911. "

25. "Annunciation Catholic [Church]." The undated clipping was found in a scrapbook belonging to Gabrielle Fraser Warren, a granddaughter of Anton Diehl (courtesy of Leland A. Dolan, Houston, Texas).

26. Delius later incorporated his *Mitternachtslied Zarathustras* into *Eine Messe des Lebens* (A mass of life) (1905). The concert was held on May 30, 1899 (not April as stated here).

27. Carley, *Delius*, 1:xxvi.

Epilogue

1. Merton, *No Man Is an Island*, xx.

2. Carley, *Delius*, 2:85.

✦ *Bibliography*

Published Sources

Beckman, Peter. *Kansas Monks: A History of St. Benedict's Abbey*. Addison, Kans.: Abbey Student Press, 1957.

Beecham, Sir Thomas. *Frederick Delius*. London: Hutchinson, 1959.

The Benedictines in Florida. Privately published pamphlet, St. Augustine Historical Society, 1940.

Bentley, George. "Tampa's Old Hotels Seem to Live On in Many Ways." *Tampa Tribune*, July 3, 1967.

Burnett, Gene M. *Florida's Past: People and Events that Shaped the State*. Englewood, Fla.: Pineapple Press, 1986.

Cahill, Mary. *Delius in Danville*. Danville, Va.: Danville Historical Society, 1986.

Carley, Lionel, ed. *Delius: A Life in Letters*, 2 vols. London: Scolar Press, 1983, 1988.

Chandler, David Leon. *Henry Flagler*. New York: Macmillan, 1986.

Chase, Gilbert. *America's Music: From the Pilgrims to the Present*. 3d ed. Urbana: University of Illinois Press, 1987.

Chop, Max. *Frederick Delius: in Monographien moderner Musiker*. 3 vols. Leipzig: C. F. Kahnt Nachfolger, 1906–9.

Cunningham, Carl. "Searching for Clues to the Last Days of One Thomas F. Ward." *Houston Post*, Jan. 29, 1989.

Danese, Emanuel. *One Hundred and Twenty-Five Years, 1854–1979: A History of the Church of the Immaculate Conception*. Jacksonville, Fla.: Privately published, [1979].

Davis, Ellis A., and Edwin H. Grobe, eds. *New Encyclopedia of Texas*. Dallas: Texas Development Bureau, 1926.

Delius, Clare. *Frederick Delius: Memories of My Brother*. London: Ivor Nicholson and Watson, 1935.

Dressman, Fr. Aloysius, ed. *St. Leo Golden Jubilee, 1890–1940*. St. Leo, Fla.: Abbey Press, 1940.

Elliott's Florida Encyclopedia or Pocket Directory. Jacksonville, Fla.: Privately published, 1889.

Fenby, Eric. *Delius*. New York: Thomas Y. Crowell, 1971.

———. *Delius as I Knew Him*. London: G. Bell and Sons, 1936.

―――. "On Delius in Florida." Program of the 24th Annual Delius Festival, Jacksonville, Fla., 1984.

Florida State Gazetter and Business Directory for 1883–84. Jacksonville, Fla.: Cushing and Appleyard, 1883.

Florida State Gazetter and Business Directory for 1884–85. Charleston, S.C.: Southern Directory Publishing, 1884.

Florida State Gazetter and Business Directory for 1886–87. Jacksonville, Fla.: John R. Richards, 1886.

Gannon, Michael. *Florida: A Short History.* Gainesville: University Press of Florida, 1993.

Grainger, Percy. "About Delius." Handscript (Photostat in Swisher Library, Jacksonville University).

―――. "The Genius of Frederick Delius." *Musical Courier* 71, no. 20 (1915): 39.

―――. "The Personality of Frederick Delius." [June 1934]. In *A Delius Companion,* edited by Christopher Palmer. London: John Calder, 1976, 117–29.

Harvey, Karen. *St. Augustine and St. Johns County: A Pictorial History.* Virginia Beach: Donning, 1980.

Hearn, Lafcadio. *Leaves from the Diary of an Impressionist.* Boston and New York: Houghton Mifflin, 1911.

Heseltine, Philip. *Frederick Delius.* London: John Lane, Bodley Head, 1923.

―――. "Some Notes on Delius and His Music." *Musical Times* 56, no. 865 (1915): 137–42. Republished in *Delius Society Journal* 94 (Autumn 1987): 3–11.

Hill, Edward Burlingame. "Frederick Delius: An Isolated Figure among New Composers." *Boston Evening Transcript,* Nov. 24, 1909.

Hitchcock, H. Wiley. *Music in the United States: A Historical Introduction.* Englewood Cliffs, N.J.: Prentice-Hall, 1969.

Hoffman, Richard. *Some Musical Recollections of Fifty Years.* New York: Charles Scribner's Sons, 1910.

Hofmann, Charles. "He [Delius] Set Florida to Music." *All Florida and TV Week Magazine,* Nov. 4, 1962, 1, 3.

Horgan, James J. *Pioneer College: The Centennial History of Saint Leo College, Saint Leo Abbey, and Holy Name Priory.* St. Leo, Fla.: St. Leo College Press, 1989.

Hueppe, Frederick Ernst. *The Radiant Light: A History of St. John's College.* Brooklyn: Privately published, 1955.

Hughes, Rupert. *Contemporary American Composers.* Boston: L. C. Page, 1900.

Humiston, William Henry. "Programme Note to Delius's Piano Concerto in C Minor." Philharmonic Society of New York, Nov. 26–27, 1915.

Hutchings, Arthur. *Delius.* London: Macmillan, 1949.

Jahoda, Gloria. "The Music-Maker of Solano Grove." In *The Other Florida.* New York: Charles Scribner's Sons, 1967, 246–69.

―――. *The Road to Samarkand.* New York: Charles Scribner's Sons, 1969.

Jefferson, Alan. *Delius.* London: J. M. Dent and Sons, 1972.

The Jesuits in Florida: Fifty Golden Years, 1889–1939. Tampa: Salesian Press, 1939.

Keany, Joseph F. *A Brief Historical Sketch of the Roman Catholic Orphan Asylum of Brooklyn.* Brooklyn: Privately published, 1930.

Kenny, Michael. "Jesuits in Our Southland, 1566–1946." Unpublished paper. Loyola University Archives, New Orleans.

Krehbiel, H. E. "A German Englishman Writes American Music." New York Tribune, Nov. 21, 1915.

Lanier, Sidney. Florida: Its Scenery, Climate, and History. Philadelphia: J. B. Lippincott, 1876.

Mason, William. Memories of a Musical Life. New York: Century, 1901.

McGrath, Father T. J. S. "Man of Vision as Seen by a Friend." Tampa Daily Times, Oct. 15, 1923.

McKay, D. B. "Pioneer Florida." Tampa Tribune, July 26, 1959.

Meany, Sister Mary Ignatius. By Railway or Rainbow. Brentwood, N.Y.: Pine Press, 1964.

Memorial of the Golden Jubilee of the Rev. Sylvester Malone. Brooklyn: Privately published, 1895.

Merton, Thomas. No Man Is an Island. New York: Harcourt Brace, 1955.

———. The Seven Storey Mountain. New York: Harcourt Brace Jovanovich, 1948.

Nolan, David. Fifty Feet in Paradise. New York: Harcourt Brace Jovanovich, 1984.

O'Brien, Lucy. Sacred Heart Parish Centennial, 1860–1960. Tampa: Privately published, 1960.

Odell, George C. D. Annals of the New York Stage. 15 vols. New York: Columbia University Press, 1927–49.

Offergeld, Robert. "Gottschalk and Company." Notes to New World Records No. NW-257, "The Wind Demon and Other Mid-19th-Century Piano Music." Ivan Davis, pianist.

Palmer, Christopher. Delius: Portrait of a Cosmopolitan. London: Gerald Duckworth, 1976.

Palmer, Edwin O. History of Hollywood. Hollywood, Calif.: Privately published, 1938.

Popular Health Resorts of the South. St. Augustine, Fla.: Chapin, [1885].

Prince, Richard E. Atlantic Coast Line Railroad Steam Locomotives, Ships and History. Salt Lake City: Privately published, 1966.

Randel, William. "Delius in America." In A Delius Companion, edited by Christopher Palmer. London: John Calder, 1976, 147–67.

———. "More on that Long-Lost Mistress." Delius Society Journal 96 (Spring 1988): 8–13.

Richards' Jacksonville City Directory. 1887. Jacksonville: John R. Richards, 1887.

Roussel, Hubert. The Houston Symphony Orchestra, 1913–1971. Austin: University of Texas Press, 1972.

Sharp, John K. History of the Diocese of Brooklyn, 1853–1953, 2 vols. Brooklyn: Roman Catholic Diocese of Brooklyn, 1954.

———. Priests and Parishes of the Diocese of Brooklyn, (1820–1944). Brooklyn: Roman Catholic Diocese of Brooklyn, 1944.

Slonimsky, Nicolas, ed. Baker's Biographical Dictionary of Musicians. 8th ed. New York: Schirmer Books, 1992.

Stiles, Henry R. The Civil, Political, Professional and Ecclesiastical History and Commercial and Industrial Record of the County of Kings and the City of Brooklyn, New York. Brooklyn: Privately published, 1884.

———. A History of the City of Brooklyn, Including the Old Town and Village of Brooklyn, the Town of Bushwick, and the Village and City of Williamsburgh. Brooklyn: Privately published, 1870.

Swinford, Sam T. "Musical Houston, 1901–1911." Houston Chronicle, Oct. 15, 1911.

Taylor, Deems. Of Men and Music. New York: Simon and Schuster, 1937.

Thomson, Bailey, and Patricia L. Meador. *Shreveport: A Photographic Remembrance, 1873–1949.* Baton Rouge: Louisiana State University Press, 1987.

Threlfall, Robert, ed. *A Catalogue of the Compositions of Frederick Delius.* London: Delius Trust, 1977. *Supplementary Catalogue,* 1986.

Ward, Thomas F. "Observer." *San Antonio (Fla.) Herald,* Apr. 15, 1892.

Webb's Historical, Industrial and Biographical Florida. New York: W. S. Webb, 1885.

Webb's Jacksonville and Consolidated Directory of the Representative Cities of East and South Florida. Jacksonville: W. S. Webb, 1886.

Williams, Grier Moffatt. "A History of Music in Jacksonville, Florida, from 1822 to 1922." Ph.D. diss., Florida State University, 1961.

Archival Sources

Annunciation Church, Houston. Archives.

Belmont Abbey, Belmont, N.C. Archives.

Brooklyn Archives of St. Francis College.

Brooklyn Historical Society.

Brooklyn Public Library Archives.

Dallas Public Library Archives.

Delius Trust, London.

Diocese of St. Augustine, Mandarin, Fla. Archives.

Grainger Museum, Melbourne.

Hillsborough County [Tampa] Historical Commission.

Hillsborough County [Tampa] Public Library.

Historic New Orleans Collection.

Houston Public Library. Texas Collection.

Jacksonville Public Library. Florida Collection; Music Collection.

Louisiana State University, Shreveport. Archives.

Loyola University Archives.

New Orleans Public Library Archives.

New-York Historical Society, New York City.

New York Public Library of the Performing Arts. Americana Collection.

Orange County History Museum, Orlando, Fla.

P. K. Yonge Library of History, University of Florida.

Queensborough Public Library, New York City.

Roman Catholic Diocese, Brooklyn, N.Y. Archives.

St. Augustine (Fla.) Historical Society.

St. James Cathedral, Brooklyn, N.Y. Archives.

St. John's University, Queens, New York. Archives.

St. Joseph's Convent, St. Augustine, Fla. Archives.

St. Leo Abbey, St. Leo, Fla. Archives.

St. Paul's Church, Brooklyn. Archives.

Swisher Library, Jacksonville University.

⇢ *Index*

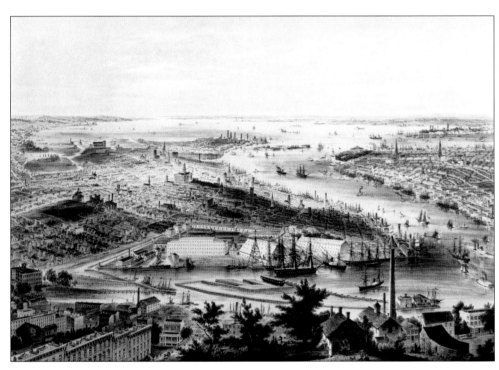

City of Brooklyn, 1855. Color lithograph by John Bornet; A. Weingarten, printer. (Brooklyn Historical Society.)

✦ *The Search for Thomas F. Ward,*

Teacher of Frederick Delius